INCIDENTS IN AN EDUCATIONAL LIFE

The University of Michigan, 1986

Incidents in an
Educational Life

A MEMOIR

(OF SORTS)

To Kathy with best wishes John Swales

John M. Swales

THE UNIVERSITY OF MICHIGAN PRESS
ANN ARBOR

This volume is largely about my professional experiences. As a result, it has little to say about my personal life. I therefore dedicate what follows to all those family members who have sustained and entertained me over the years. They are—in order of occurrence—the Swales family, the Aizlewoods, the Smiths, the Jabados, and the Benners.

CONTENTS

PREFACE

In this smallish book, I recount a number of incidents from my educational life, starting with my oldest memory of my kindergarten days in about 1942 and ending (more or less) with my final official retirement in 2007. I retell most of these remembered incidents in the form of vignettes, some of which would purport to be unusual, and at times perhaps even bizarre, some purport to be entertaining, but many others to offer some kind of educational message, however small and incidental. A few of these last I have already discussed in usually a more formal and succinct way in print or in various talks or lectures.

So, this is the kind of little volume that ought by rights to be published privately or, as I suppose in 21st-century style, to be self-published. In some ways then, a collection of reminiscences and reflections to be foisted on unsuspecting friends, colleagues and relatives. On the other hand, several readers of draft chapters, including Kelly Sippell of the University of Michigan Press, have suggested that there are elements in the work that might have wider appeal; hence its appearance under the UM Press imprint. In the end, I hope particularly that there are, within these confines, some narrated experiences that may resonate with others who have pursued comparable educational lives as teachers, lecturers or volunteers, or with younger people who might be interested in how things were in my own areas of endeavor at various times in the past.

I have conceived these vignettes of my "educational life" fairly broadly, but I have usually refrained from discussing any intersections there might have been with romantic attachments, family involvements, or political beliefs. Although these are doubtless all part of a fuller autobiography, I have chosen to focus on those incidents in an educational life that might seem—for the most part—to cast light on one individual's history as a teacher, materials designer, researcher and writer in ways that might conceivably be of interest to others.

I have used British style (including punctuation conventions) for the years up to my move to the United States at the end of 1984, and American style for the years thereafter. Since this is not an academic book, I have not included chapter and verse for the numerous quoted extracts, nor have I attempted a close transliteration of the Arabic names.

I am grateful to all those who have read and commented on parts of the manuscript, and particularly grateful to Vi Benner and Theresa Rohlck for their close readings of all the manuscript chapters. I would also like to thank Oxford University Press for permission to include an extract from *The Memoirs of Babiker Bedri*.

INCIDENTS IN AN EDUCATIONAL LIFE

ONE

Schoolboy Years

1

The Motorcycle

My earliest educational memory is of going to kindergarten. (I have earlier memories, such as my father, home on leave, taking me out at night to hear the German bombers going over our house some 25 miles south of central London.) The kindergarten was run by a stout elderly lady called Mrs Lloyd. As memory goes, she always wore long black dresses and was always kindly but firm. In 1942, petrol was not available for the general public, and so Mrs Lloyd used to round up her small charges in the morning and dispatch them close to their homes in the early afternoon in a pony-and-trap. In addition to the obvious adventure of this mode of transport (an occasional fallen apple for the pony), there was the "motorcycle". In actual fact, this was a short, very narrow bench fixed onto the floor of the trap to accommodate various extra small bodies. I remember the competition to ride on the motorcycle, rather than on the traditional trap seats. The journeys to and from school were quite long, and often cold and wet, but all was forgotten if you were lucky enough to get a spot on the "motorbike".

I don't remember too much else of these first educational experiences. The "school" took place in a church hall and on fine days we would all sit on thick rubber mats with circular holes in them on the grass outside. (Why should I remember that?) There is also a photo of me at age three or four dressed up as a pixie for some end-of-term show. What I do remember is an interview I had, accompanied by my mother, at the end of my kindergarten years with some elderly lady who was checking out my educational accomplishments to date. After she had established that I could read the simple children's books that she had brought with her, she turned to multiplication tables. And here, readers need to remember that in the England of those days we still had a system of 12 pennies to a shilling and 20 shillings to a pound. So, every child in the country had to learn multiplication tables from 1 to 12, for how else would they be able to cope with the money system? So, I answered all the questions (8 times 4? 12 times 12?) fine, and then came the real cruncher, the 7-times table. (For some reason, for many children this was the tricky one, perhaps because it was furthest from the obvious benchmark five-times and ten-times tables.) I clearly remember the proud look on my mother's face when I immediately responded to the devilish "7 times 7?" with the appropriate "49".

2

A beating and a bullying

The next stage in my education was my attending a "prep" or preparatory school, so called because it was designed to prepare the boys (and yes, we were all boys) for the Common Entrance examinations for the Public Schools—a misnomer since they were typically expensive, private boarding schools, nearly all single sex. I was a day-boy not a boarder at one such prep school, a 20-minute bus ride from my home. The headmaster and owner of the school was rather elderly and not in good health, and I now suspect the school was going downhill at least in terms of maintenance, heating, sanitation and things like that. In those years of the middle 1940s, it was certainly cold because coal was scarce and the winters at that time were much harsher than they are to-day. However, the school must have been academically strong, because quite often a half-holiday would be announced after one of the senior boys had won a scholarship to some prestigious public school.

One incident I remember was the day when the whole of my class (some fifteen eight-year-olds I would guess) were each given three strokes of the cane on our behinds because we had all singularly failed to be able to conjugate the present tense of *être*. We lined up outside the headmaster's study to receive punishment for this morphological ab-jectness—punishment to be administered by our French teacher and the second master, Mr Shegog. We small boys were fascinated by this weird name, but I have since discovered that it is not so rare and, in fact, quite widespread; for instance, about a decade later I was surprised and intrigued that there was a Reverend Shegog in Faulkner's *The Sound and the Fury*. I mention this incident because this was the only time I was beaten for academic delinquency. Some time after this inci-dent, I believe Mr Shegog ran away from the school in the company of the school matron.

The other series of incidents that remain clear in my mind from this school probably do so because it was the only time that I was seriously bullied. It came about like this. One day, the rather frail headmaster an-nounced at school lunchtime that the annual school photograph might not be possible this year because a key piece was missing from the school's pre-war German camera, for which of course in the 1940s there were no spare parts—and had anybody seen it? At which, a couple of boys said, "Swales has been playing with it". At that time, and to this day, I have no recollection of ever having handled the release mecha-nism or whatever it was, but I promised to look through my toys at home to see if I could find it. I guess I did so, even if somewhat half-heartedly, knowing that I was innocent. But for several subsequent weeks, I was set upon by groups of older boys as I walked up the school drive in the morning. Pushed, shoved, and shouted at—"Haven't you found it yet? We have no school photograph because of you, Swales" and so forth. In consequence, for those weeks, I grew fearful, and at times tearful, at the prospect of having to go to school, although I never told my parents about the trouble I was in. Eventually, of course, the harassment died away and I was left in peace for my remaining time at the school.

Several years later, we moved to a larger house in another part of town, and I was asked to clear out my toy cupboard taking only those toys that were still of interest to me. Right at the back of this cupboard I found a small, black-painted bit of metal with a short length of red ribbon attached to it. The missing piece of the camera! I confess my emotions were pretty mixed on this discovery. Late in life (or so I presume), I have become an avid and appreciative reader of the short stories by that great Irish short-story writer, William Trevor, so here is how William Trevor might have closed his account of these events:

> It is odd that guilt doesn't always lead to shame, or indeed shame to guilt. Indeed, tossing that small piece of hapless tin into the box along with the other discarded toys, broken or excessively childish, even seemed to that small boy a mild retribution of sorts.

3

A horrible school and its aftermath

When I had reached the ripe old age of nine or so, my parents decided that it was time for me to endure the rigors of boarding school. They probably felt that the school I had been attending was lacking somewhat in sanitation, nutrition and the like, so they sent me to a school on the south coast of England. This school was run by two brothers, both of whom had been majors in the army, and they ran the school—perhaps in consequence—with great discipline as represented by a huge number of arcane rules. For one example, there were painted lines on many of the floors, and only third-years could cross red lines, and fourth-years blue lines, while first-years like me could hardly cross any lines at all! Worse, I was placed in the bottom class because I was new, even though I was older than most of the others in it. One of these majors took us for geography, and one day asked us what kinds of power there were. I answered with something like "wind power, water power, steam power, hydro-electric power, internal combustion power". I would like to think I would have added "nuclear power", although that might have been a bit prescient because I don't think the first nuclear power station in Britain was yet in operation. But I could see that the major, far from being pleased with my impressive answer, hated me for it. After all, I had ruined his apparent lesson plan of slowly extracting from his reluctant pupils all the kinds of power he had in mind. (There is a lesson here for teachers about the dangers of asking that kind of open question, especially if there is a smart-alec or two in the class, rather than elicitations of the form "Can you tell me *one* kind of power?")

After several weeks, I came to dislike everything about this school, the stupid regimentation, the overly easy boring lessons, the determination of the ex-military co-head and geography teacher to put me in my place. So, one morning, in a sort of desperation, I went to the school matron and pretended to be feeling ill; a day in the sick-bay, I thought, would be much better than a day in the tedious classes. So that afternoon, the school doctor came by and examined his new patient. To my growing anxiety, he spent an inordinate amount of time banging away on my chest and asking me to cough. "Christ", I thought, "I'm in even more trouble now; I have been found out as a malingerer". (Though, I doubt if I knew that word then.) Anyway, the next thing I knew I was being wheeled into an ambulance and on my way to Hastings General Hospital, and, as we went down the drive, the last I ever saw of that horrible school was the white faces of a number of small boys staring excitedly out of the schoolroom windows at this dramatic turn of events.

I spent six months in the hospital because it turned out that, far from feigning illness, I had contracted "pleurisy with tubercular complications". I suspect in the first months I was in fact quite ill because I remember the matron of the hospital (an august personage indeed) used to stop by my bed with a few soft encouraging words on her evening rounds. Once we started to improve, on sunny winter days, we T.B. patients used to be wheeled out onto the balcony in our beds. My neighbor in the children's ward was a girl a couple of years older than me, and we became quite friendly. Because of my segregated education, this was the first time I could actually talk to a girl (my younger sister didn't of course count); moreover, she came from a large working-class family in the local town. So I could learn much from what she said about what they ate, what they did on Sundays, and so on. Once, probably when she was feeling particularly friendly, she offered to show me her budding breast, but this was at night in the ward and I couldn't see anything but a vague white blur.

The other main educational benefit of this hospital stay was my discovery of children's novels. I came to have two favorite authors; my number one was Malcolm Saville and number two was Arthur Ransome (number two because some of his books were very long—like Harry Potter). Both were regional English writers with a very strong sense of the regional countryside, such as the Welsh border, the Lake District and the Norfolk Broads, and their novels contained coteries of children and a range of exciting but plausible adventures that a ten-year-old boy in a hospital bed could identify with. In fact, I recently re-read, after nearly 60 years, one novel from each author (Saville's *Strangers at Snowfell* and Ransome's *Coot Club*); I have to confess that I found both just as good as I remembered them. I was therefore not totally surprised to recently discover that both authors, although Ransome died in 1967 and Saville in 1982, are remembered by lively societies in their names on the web, which offer various kinds of events and activities suitable for fans of many ages.

I returned home after six months, but only to my upstairs bedroom where I was to remain for a further four or five months. After a time, my parents realized that card games, chess, stamp collecting and children's novels did not quite make up for the loss of a whole school year. So they hired a retired mathematics teacher to come and give me lessons. This was a Mr Ede, who had a large, beaky and colorful nose, but Mr Ede was also a great teacher of geometry, and, as best I recollect, we worked our way through the first three books of Euclid. I particularly enjoyed the circle theorems, and toward the end Mr Ede would sometimes draw a circle with associated tangents and then ask me what problem could be set based on this figure. I had the first glimmerings on these occasions of the challenges such role-reversals could provide—an issue I will return to once or twice more in the following pages.

4

Beyond my limited powers

When I was back on my feet, I went as a day-boy to a different preparatory school on the other side of my home town, and life there was fairly uneventful for the next two or three years as I prepared for the Common Entrance Examination for one of the so-called Public Schools. (I made some friends, played a bit of sport, had my appendix out, and was usually close to the top of the class in most subjects.) Indeed, in my final year, the headmaster, doubtless in a fit of ill-considered enthusiasm, decided I should sit for the Winchester scholarship exam. (This was a school, unlike my first prep school, that never won scholarships, and considered itself lucky if it could get its pupils accepted at middle-rank public schools.) So, the time came for the Winchester Scholarship papers. Now, Winchester College, at least at that time, was regarded as the "brainiest" Public School, its graduates going on to occupy the highest ranks of the Government's Civil Service; these were the so-called "mandarins", the Permanent Under-Secretaries who ran the various ministries; these were the guys who could sit on the train on their morning commutes to central London and complete *The Times'* cryptic crossword by the time they were half-way there.

Some of the papers weren't too bad, history, English, math (at least the geometry questions!), and I sat several hours a day, a very inky 12-year old, alone in one of the upstairs dormitories with the local vicar acting as invigilator/proctor. Then came the day for the "Latin Verse Paper". I opened it, and it said "Translate the following poem into iambic pentameters". "Ye gods", I thought, "I'm not ready for this". I had, by this time, read and translated a little Latin poetry, such as Virgil's famous opening passage in the Aeniad that begins *Arma virumque cano*. I had had a little practice in scanning Latin verse, marking it into short and long syllables (spondees and trochees and the like), and even had a vague idea (no clearer today) of what a *caesura* was. But writing the stuff! I supposed that there were force-fed brainy boys out there who could rise to this challenge, but at Hillside School I wasn't one of them.

I then turned to the English poem I had to translate into Latin verse, and I couldn't even make much sense of the source text. I remember it was a short poem by William Savage Landor, an early 19th-century poet and maverick. I can't remember the exact poem now, but let us imagine it was this one—a six-liner by W. S. Landor:

> THE DUKE OF YORK'S STATUE
> *Enduring is the bust of bronze,*
> *And thine, Oh flower of George's sons,*
> *Stand high above all laws and duns.*
> *As honest men as ever cart*
> *Convey'd to Tyburn took thy part*
> *And raised thee up to where thou art.*

Was this the Duke of York who had ten thousand men? And what on earth were those "duns"? ("Could they be soldiers dressed in khaki? No, soldiers didn't wear khaki then."). Next, I couldn't parse the complex syntax of Lines 4 and 5, and I thought Tyburn was where criminals were taken to be hanged, so what was this stuff about "honest men". Over the next two hours, I translated the title and nothing else, mainly because I belatedly remembered that the Roman name for York was "Eboracum".

Of course, I got nowhere with the scholarship, nor with my parents' hopes of me entering the prestigious Winchester College as a simple "commoner", although I did scrape into a minor public school called Lancing College, more on which to come. However, one educational incident did arise from this debacle that was highly instructive. The headmaster, probably realizing that he had put me in an impossible position with the Winchester Scholarship, asked me one day toward the end of my final year to accompany him to the splendid independent bookshop in town (still there I am very glad to say) in order to select the school prizes. In his car on the way there, he said, "Swales, you are pretty good at history; please choose six history prize books for the best history students in each of the six years, and then choose one for yourself." I think for the first time in my life I had to think of audience and reception (except for pathetic attempts to find Christmas presents for my mother). I pondered what boys aged seven to twelve would like, and eventually made choices that met with his approval. For myself, I chose a pictorial history of the kings and queens of England since at that time I had memorized all their names and dates. Like nearly all the boys, I liked Mr B. the headmaster; he was large man with a jovial outward-going personality, and with a terrific outdoor model railway set-up next to the vegetable garden. So, I was more than pleased with his approbation, and at the prize-giving ceremony, before the assembled boys, parents and siblings, I was not so much gratified with the prizes I received, but more with the announcement of the history prizes, and my secret pride in the fact that I had chosen them.

Some years later, Mr B. died prematurely of a heart attack—or so I believe—and the school went out of business, the buildings were demolished, and it and its extensive sports grounds were transformed into what the British are pleased to call "a housing estate".

5

Traveling the East Coast Main

During my pre-teen years, I used to go to stay with my grandfather and grandmother for a week or so each early September in their house in Scarborough on the Yorkshire coast. My grandfather had bought a house there after he retired as the Chief Water Engineer for the City of Sheffield. The main event of these visits was attending the Scarborough Cricket Festival with my grandparents, but the main educational incidents occurred on the journey there. My father used to take me by car to King's Cross Station in London and put me on the train for Scotland, and my grandparents used to meet me off the train at the wonderful railway station in York and then drive the forty miles or so to Scarborough.

For the journeys up and down, I had somehow acquired a remarkable pamphlet which I think was called the *Main Line North*; I have a clearer memory of its author, a certain Major Pike M.B.E. It was in the form of those specialized maps that motoring organizations sometimes provide, in which the route to be taken takes up some 20 pages, always starting at the bottom and ending at the top. So this was a route map made to entertain and educate the general public about the railroad from London to Edinburgh. It showed all the junctions, marshalling yards, bridges and speed restrictions, and everything else that somebody might like to know. I remember, for instance, the 30 mph restriction as the train encountered the sharp bends on its approach to Peterborough. (Doubtless long since smoothed out.)

The best thing about the booklet, however, was its detailed accounts of the high-speed sections. It announced that the section started at such a landmark, such as a level crossing, and ended a few miles down the line at another landmark, such as a bridge across a river. And the really best thing about Major Pike's work was that these high-speed sections were accompanied by little charts that converted your timing in seconds between the two landmarks into the speed of the train in miles per hour. The first of these, as best I recall, occurred somewhere not too far north of London between Hitchin and Hatfield. So, I would time the section and note the speed obtained on the conversion chart. (I think 89 mph was the fastest I ever found.) Naturally, this small boy's industrious activity excited the curiosity of some of the other passengers in the compartment. Only *some* mind you—for some strange reason none of the female passengers ever took much interest. On the other hand, men, especially middle-aged men, would soon have their watches out, scanning the passing countryside as they waited for the next high speed section. Often they would inquire where I got the pamphlet, but I never really knew. On one remembered occasion, a military-officer type sitting in a corner seat and observing our antics barked out, "You need to synchronize your watches". "Synchronize your watches!"—that's what they said in the war-films of the time as our intrepid heroes made final preparations to leave on some important but highly dangerous mission! My day was made.

Many cultures have sayings and expressions that stress the close relationship between travel and learning, and certainly from those days on the East Coast Main, I have been a keen observer of the passing scene, especially when traveling by train or bus. Recently, I have been trying to find a copy of Major Pike's valuable educational contribution, but to no avail. And when I notice the traveling children of today absorbed in their iPods or electronic games, I often wish they could have bought at the station bookshop just such a pamphlet so they too could time the high-speed sections.

6

Three memorable educational experiences
and a good piece of advice

So let's fast-forward a couple of years, and I am now doing quite well at my public school with its strong Anglican tradition (compulsory Chapel every day and twice on Sundays). I had started out as a 13-year-old in the next to bottom class because of my indifferent Common Entrance examination performance, but my second year I got promoted at Christmas to the class occupied by my brighter co-evals. During this year we had to have a compulsory art class once a week which was taught, as it happened, by my housemaster. He was always known as "Utter Parsons" because every time some small boy stammered out excuses for some sin of omission or commission, he always used to respond with this dismissive rejoinder—"Utter balls!" Anyway, in his art class, we were supposed to draw and paint various things, one I remember being to design a record sleeve for our favorite record. As it happened, toward the end of the school year the headmaster had issued an edict that all classes were to have a final exam. Our art teacher objected strongly, arguing that art couldn't be measured in this way. However, the headmaster prevailed and Utter Parsons entered the exam hall with our art exam papers. To our great surprise, he handed out blank sheets of paper and then, scowling, wrote on the blackboard: "Construct six examination questions and answer two of them".

This was one of those challenges—like choosing the history prizes—that put me, and I expect others of my classmates, in a "new place". We had suddenly to think like grown-ups, like teachers; we had to try to be excessively clever and yet not totally far-fetched; we also had to learn to think carefully about the wording of the questions. At this distance, I can only remember one topic I chose, which I suspect went something like this:

> To what extent do you think the design of a record cover sleeve can affect sales?

But I do remember that this was one of the questions that I didn't attempt to answer myself! And I also remember the excitement of my classmates as we left the examining hall, chattering among ourselves about the brilliant questions we had come up with.

A term or so later I found myself in the top set (or 'track' in U.S. parlance) for Latin, when we were to experience for the first time the redoubtable senior Latin teacher. Now, Latin in those days had a fixed methodology known as "construing". We were assigned to prepare for homework a certain number of lines from the Latin author we were studying, and in class, and in turn, each boy would be assigned to read aloud a sentence and then translate it. Then the next boy would deal similarly with the next sentence, and so on around the class, interspersed with occasional interventions by the teacher about some particularly succulent piece of grammar or some arcane allusion to a Roman historical or mythological figure. Given this fixed methodology, all depended then on the Latin author that the instructor had chosen. As the top set, and after about five years of Latin, we were expecting some middlingly difficult author like Livy or Cicero. So, in came the redoubtable Mr Handford who handed out the worn and palimpsested set textbooks for the term. It was Julius Caesar's *Gallic Wars* (and invasion of Britain), the easiest Latin author of all! This was going to be a piece of cake!

Mr Handford, after a few opening remarks, got us to open the textbooks at the first Latin passage, and some boy was asked to begin. He read aloud the first sentence and then paused in preparation for translating. He was waved on to read the next . . . and then the next . . . and then the next. Even we callous school boys began to think "poor bugger, having to translate all that, and unseen too" (i.e. without prior preparation). When he got to the end of the first page, Mr Handford then mildly inquired—and here came one of the biggest educational shocks in my life—"Any questions?" It dawned on us that we were being expected to follow the Latin without translating it. And, in fact, this turned out to be a marvelous class with us using the Latin to reconstruct a documentary account of Caesar's military campaigns, and Mr Handford guiding our efforts with his historical maps and enlivening the general's descriptions with vignettes of life in the Roman Empire. It transpired that I would continue with Latin for almost the rest of my schooldays, but the later texts were never easier enough for me to read without translating or having to consult translations. So, the educational lessons I later took from Mr Handford's class were that easy texts in a foreign language could lead to sophisticated tasks, that teaching reading was very different from testing it, and more generally, that there were clear advantages in 'biasing for success' in pedagogical endeavors.

At about this time I went through a religious phrase, among other things becoming a server for communion in the large and famous college chapel. As part of this experience, one Sunday, two or three other boys and I accompanied the chaplain (wearing his best cassock) in his rickety old car to a nunnery some 30 miles away. He was going to collect a new altar cloth that the nuns had been embroidering. By the time we had had tea and extolled the beauty of the embroidery, we were running late because the chaplain had to be back before six in order to conduct the Sunday evening service, the most important one of the week.

In his haste, he drove through a red light and was stopped by a policeman on a motorcycle. As the officer approached, he stuck his head out of the window and breathlessly asked, "I am on the right way to the hospital?" The policeman immediately waved him on and we sped off. In the ensuing silence, the chaplain explained at great length that he had not in fact uttered a falsehood of any kind, but merely used his clerical authority in such a way that he wouldn't be late for chapel. I recollect over the next days, having earnest discussions about the Christian ethics of the Chaplain's question with another server who was something of a friend—without any clear result. However, this exposure to questionable ethical behavior on the part of an ordained member of the Church of England did not prevent me from knocking on his study door one evening some time later. As he opened it, I said, "Good evening, sir. I think I have received the call to the priesthood". He looked at me wisely and replied, "Don't be silly, Swales. Go away". One of the best pieces of advice I have ever received.

7

Into rarified atmospheres

After my short flirtation with the religious life, I turned into a committed pseudo-intellectual, writing modernist poetry and reading Virginia Woolf's *Mrs Dalloway* sitting uncomfortably up in a tree. Ah, the physical discomforts we aesthetes have to endure! I was also reading William Faulkner, and I note that my battered and oil-marked hard copy (it bounced around in the boot/trunk of my car on various moves) of *The Sound and the Fury* is dated below my signature as "Feb, 1955". I doubt if many 16-year-old British teenagers were reading Faulkner in the middle 1950s. A strong impetus to these literary aspirations was the arrival of a new sixth form English and History teacher, Roger Lockyer, who would later go on to be a Reader in History at the University of London. For example, he used to take a bunch of us sixth formers to the Quaker Meeting House in the nearby city of Brighton, where, on one memorable occasion, I heard Elizabeth Jennings read her poetry. The Meeting House had a large laundry basket which operated as a book exchange; one placed a volume in and took a volume for borrowing out. On the occasion I remember I put my hand deep into the basket's recesses and pulled out Joyce's *Finnegan's Wake*, a clear enough sign of the literary aspirations of the organization. After a brief scrutiny, I selected something else. Many years later, I came across a comment Joyce made about his final work; it went something like "It took me 19 years to write it, so I don't see why it shouldn't take you 19 years to read it". Well, in 1955, I didn't have those years.

I was now a sixth-former and preparing for the university entrance A/S level examinations. One of my subjects was *History in Foreign Texts*. This was a short-lived experiment to add a second History "A Level", requiring students to read history in two languages other than English, one ancient (Latin or Greek) and one modern (French or German). We were a small group of four, as best I remember, who embarked on this odyssey. The French texts were written by Voltaire and Michelet, and didn't present too much of a problem. The Latin texts were typically Tacitus for classical Latin and Eginhard's *Life of Charlemagne* for mediaeval Latin. Tacitus is always tough since he wrote in a brilliant but extremely terse style somewhat reminiscent of the *Time/Newsweek* manner of political reporting. Translations were, of course, available. Our teacher, a Mr Ray, however decided that this year he was tired of the standard Eginhard and he would opt for the alternate mediaeval text, *A Life of King Canute and a Eulogy of his Wife Emma*, written by some monk in 11th century Iceland. The first problem arose when our texts eventually arrived from Hamburg and we discovered that all the notes were in German, of which I (for one) knew not a word. Additionally, the text turned out to be extremely obscure, not so much in the descriptions of King Canute's military and political conquests, nor in the accounts of the good deeds of his wife Emma, but in the depictions of the details of the Viking ships, their journeys, and their navigational techniques. None of our dictionaries could deal with this lexicon. However, the teaching staff rose to the challenge. I clearly remember a meeting of us quartet of boys, the senior German teacher, all the Latin teachers, a meeting even graced by the austere, scholarly presence of the head-master, and all designed to "crack" the difficult passages. With this in-terdisciplinary team on board, all of us sixth-formers "aced", as the Americans say, both the translation and essay questions on the exami-nation. I think we all achieved the much-desired "S" for scholarship level in our results. An early indication perhaps of the value of inter-disciplinary teams, but also a demonstration of how a closed commu-nity of quasi-academics (we were all stuck on a hill a few miles from the local fleshpots) could rise to the occasion. A lesson I carried with me when, as we will see, I was surprisingly appointed head of the English section at the College of Engineering at the University of Libya in 1966.

For our main history A/S level we had two teachers of contrasting styles, not unlike the two depicted in Alan Bennett's *The History Boys*, the younger one being the Roger Lockyer I have already mentioned. It was he who mostly trained us to write essays in the standard examina-tion format of those days (write four essays in three hours out of a choice of a dozen or so). Since most of the essay questions were of the *discuss* type, he emphasized the need for strong argument supported by historical detail (ideally involving contemporary quotations). He also stressed sentence variation and impressive choice of words and en-couraged us, very unusually at that time, to rewrite our essays. Our ef-forts he meticulously commented on, sometimes in a rather oblique kind of way when he would write in the margin "how would the ex-aminers respond to this argument?" Like the younger master in *The History Boys*, he wanted intellectually imaginative answers to the ques-tions, rather than ones that offered sober historical description.

Among the smallish group of history sixth-formers was a remark-able boy some two years younger than the rest of us. This was Francis and he was perhaps the only genius I have ever known. The history masters were always reading parts of his essays out to the rest of us be-cause they were full of fancy but useful historical words like *nadir* and *apogee*. After we had done our A levels, Francis and I were prepared for the Oxford and Cambridge Scholarship examinations, Francis going to Oxford and me to Cambridge. I got some of the questions I wanted, es-pecially ones on feudalism, the mediaeval wool trade, and the "new men" brought in by Henry VIII, and for this last I could use the telling quotation from Sir Thomas Browne that I can remember to this day: "Where is Bohun, where is Mortimer, nay, what is more and most of all, where is Plantagenet? They are entombed in the urns and sepulchres of mortality". But I didn't get a question about English-Dutch naval rivalry in the late 17th and early 18th centuries, where my argument for the gradual rise in British seapower hinged on the movement of North Sea herrings from off the Dutch coast to the Scottish one, and for which I had a contemporary quotation in Dutch with an English translation. (That one I don't now remember.) During my three-day stay at Queens' College Cambridge, I had an interview with Peter Matthias, the senior history tutor and a great economic historian, who—as I soon discovered—had had the dubious privilege of reading my essays. He focused on my essay on the mediaeval wool trade, the question for which had gone something like "What were the probable causes of the move of the wool manufacturing industry from east of England to the west of England in the fifteenth century?" I had answered, cleverly I thought, that the principal reason for the migration was the better and faster sources of water in the western hills. Dr. Matthias queried this by pointing out that his researches had shown that the water-intensive fulling part of the operation would account for at most 10% of the production cost and so that couldn't be the principal reason. "What other explanation do you have, Mr Swales?" I sat there in his oak-panelled and book-lined study at a total loss for words. "Done for", I said to myself as I stumbled out.

Although most of the scholarship exams consisted of writing four essays in three hours, there was also a single long essay section where we were supposed to write on one topic for three hours. Francis at Christchurch, Oxford, chose to write on this question:

> The reformation did not take place in Wittenberg or Geneva but in Lausanne and Cambridge. Discuss.

The point of this question would be that Luther at Wittenberg and Calvin at Geneva were essentially mediaeval in their thinking, and that the real reformers came along later. Francis, in his usual fluent style, wrote for three hours on the topic, answering it in this way: The proposition is correct because the reformation is a figment of the imagination of two famous late 19th-century historians, Professor Burckhardt of the University of Lausanne and Lord Acton of the University of Cambridge.

This was of course *un grand coup* of huge proportions and Francis was offered the top scholarship in history at all the colleges who had seen his papers. He couldn't go up at the end of the year because he was still fifteen at the time. He spent a year in Paris with some relatives and then, or so I believe, he secretly (and illegally) enrolled full-time at both Oxford and at London, where he studied Chinese. He finished up before he was 20 with two good second-class degrees, but then apparently died in Paris a few years later. It would be easy enough to conclude this story of Francis with something like "those whom the gods love die young", but I will refrain, merely reiterating that, although I have met many very clever people in my life, only Francis would I put into the category of "genius".

8

An early taste of realpolitik

By the time of the Cambridge Scholarship, I had risen high in the school. I was head of my house (there were seven houses at the time), a school prefect, in fact deputy head boy, and I had also been getting my first teaching experience. I was a sergeant in the College Cadet Force and used to teach fieldcraft on Friday afternoons to the younger boys—mostly map reading plus some stealth manoeuvres such as the Ghost Walk and the Monkey Run. Or was it the Ghost Run and the Monkey Walk?

I was puzzled then on my return from Cambridge to find my house prefects' common room deserted and the younger boys looking at me silently and sidling off. I was called to the housemaster's office where I soon learnt what had happened whilst I was away. The house prefects and I had bought an old tiny Austin Seven car for $20, which we kept stashed in a local wood and used on occasion to make an evening run to a nearby village pub (but not the closest one to the school for that was the locale to which the masters would repair after a hard day's schoolmastering). All this was of course totally against the school rules; worse, none of us had a driving license and the car was neither registered nor insured. Anyway, our escapade was discovered during my absence in the Fens of Cambridgeshire, all the house prefects were expelled, and the car on the weekend was unceremoniously towed away by one of the fathers in front of an excited crowd of younger boys. I was immediately sent to the headmaster who, after giving me a thorough tongue-lashing, ruefully admitted that he couldn't expel me too, because then he would have nobody left to run Seconds House. Ah, that early lesson in *realpolitik*! My punishment, if that's what it was, was to be disinvited from reading the school prefect's lesson at the Christmas Carol Service. Towards the end of this sticky interview, he inquired as to how I had got on at Cambridge. Remembering my pathetic performance in the study of the senior history tutor, I mumbled something about "not as well as I'd hoped." "A pity", said the headmaster, because Oxbridge scholarships did much to boost a school's reputation, "but maybe there's an outside chance for an exhibition". (Exhibitions being the lowest of the three scholarship classes, the top one being a major scholarship, which of course Francis got.)

A few days into the Christmas holidays I got a telegram at home from Queens' College stating that I had been awarded a minor scholarship in history worth 60 pounds a year, and the next day both the headmaster and Roger Lockyer telephoned me to offer their congratulations. They had seen the announcement in *The Times*. Unfortunately, the news came too late for my grandfather, who had always followed my academic career with great interest, since he had died a few months earlier. As my mother noted, he would have been particularly pleased.

9

Proxime accessit

My final term at school left me with rather little to do. I would go "up" (as they say) to Cambridge in the autumn and, because I had won a scholarship, I didn't have to do National Military Service first. I therefore decided to enter for a number of the open-competition annual school prizes. Although I hadn't done any science for years, I decided to enter for the Biology Prize since the subject seemed to be the manageable "Soil Erosion". I entered the local bishop's theology essay prize on the topic of whether the Church of England should be disestablished as the country's official religion, and I entered the Leonardo general knowledge prize. When the results were posted on one of the official notice boards, I was placed *proxime accessit* (runner-up) in each case. The Biology Prize was awarded to a boy whose father worked as a consultant on soil erosion in the Middle East, and the theology prize was awarded to the son of a bishop! The Leonardo Prize was given to a friend of mine called David Barwell, who went up to Oxford and then entered the Foreign Service. (The last time I met him he was press officer in the British Embassy in Cairo.) One of the examiners later told me I might have won the Leonardo if I had not made a botch of one of the music questions. These were short answer responses to composer's names and a comment about them. My downfall was: "Grieg: 'A pink fondant stuffed with snow'. Discuss". Alas, I didn't know what a "fondant" was and consequently wrote some rubbish about the pink fountains of Norway. The laughter in the masters' common room at this gaffe didn't apparently forward my case, or so my informant told me.

10

An Italian adventure

The other event of my final term was that I was awarded, as a result of the Cambridge success, a school travel scholarship for 50 pounds. I decided to go for two months to the University for Foreigners at Perugia in central Italy. This would be the first time I would be outside the British Isles—the furthest I had been so far was a cycling holiday in Ireland—and I was both excited and nervous about the whole venture. I studied the Teach-Yourself-Italian book and my father found me a tutor in a local town, whom I would visit once a week. The tutor also arranged for me to stay three weeks with an elderly couple in Vicenza in the Po valley before going to Perugia. On the train there I remember practicing sotto voce such momentous utterances as *la prossima stazione è Vicenza?* and *Cerco la Viale Bonomo* (the address of the lawyer and his wife). Eventually I found my way to the viale and introduced myself to la signora, who showed me to my attic bedroom (which turned out to be very hot and somewhat mosquito-infested). The signora soon took advantage of my presence and young, elegant and sometimes glamorous young ladies of the city (always alas in dutiful twos) would come round for private lessons in English from il signorino Inglese. I can't remember much of these, except that a lot of giggling went on among my pupils, and that reading a children's version of Cinderella as part of the signora's curriculum for improving my Italian—was not a very good choice, I thought.

After two weeks or so, the elderly couple announced they had to go away for reasons that never became clear, but then added that they had made arrangements for me to stay in the local monastery for a week. This turned out to be a rare order established in the 19th century by Cardinal Newman. The abbot in charge was an educated and intelligent man, but most of the 20 or so brothers were an eye-opening lot; two or three were too fond of wine and efforts (often unsuccessful) were made to try and ensure that the wine decanter did not stay long

21

with them as it made the evening rounds; a couple of others tended to over-indulge when the food platters circulated, leaving almost nothing for lesser mortals such as myself. The only young brother showed me his girlie magazines, and took me on the back of his Vespa on his visits to the local tobacco-farmers, where we used in each case to pass half an hour or so sampling the hapless farmer's home-made liquor. And finally, there was the monastery doctor, a morose southern Italian, who explained to me that southern Italian medical schools produced far too many doctors and this was the only job he could get—room and board, both pretty indifferent, and a derisory monthly stipend of 14,000 lire (perhaps two pounds a week). All in all, my short spell in the monastery was an entry into a kind of Bruegelesque world, in which the peccadillos of its inmates made my school chaplain's equivocations about his question to the police patrolman seem rather arcane.

Once in Perugia, I found myself largely in the company of older people. The fellow student in the next room to me was a 40-year-old French translator for the United Nations, and in the same block were two Americans, both in their thirties I would now suspect, who were still eking out a fairly idle existence on the G.I. Bill. Although at least one of them spoke pretty passable Italian, they both had opted for the beginners' class because, as they later explained me, that was where the fanciable Northern European women tended to congregate. Listening to these guys talk about their experiences was another eye-opener for me.

The Frenchman and I attended the intermediate class which was taught by a small rotund professor with a great eye for detail; indeed, one of his favorite topics was how to correctly divide Italian words when you got to the end of the line. Since I was still struggling with basic morphology and sentence structure, I eventually found these kinds of minutiae of little relevance. Instead, in my final month, I opted for a short content course on Etruscology. I chose this because we were promised lots of pictures, two guided tours of the city and a trip to a famous Etruscan well. At least, I thought I could get something from the visuals, even if much of the lectures would go over my head. And so it proved. Further, in one of those quirks of circumstance, my short *Etrus-*

cologia experience almost certainly helped me to land my first job (as will doubtless be revealed).

Perugia was very cheap in those days and we could afford to eat in the evening in the small local *trattorie*, where groups of us would argue about politics, films, books, places and people until late in the evening. There is only one ostensibly trivial discussion that I clearly remember. We had all been earlier to see an American western, which was as usual dubbed into Italian. At one moment in the film, the hero enters the bar in a town dominated by some bad guys and asks for a whisky. The barman, doubtless in thrall to the bad guys, pays no notice and continues to polish glasses at the other end of the counter. Our hero repeats his request for a drink, but again gets no response. So he strolls down the counter to the barman, grabs him by his jacket and yells at him in Italian, "Don't you understand English?" The Frenchman and I start laughing our heads off, but nobody else in the party or elsewhere in the cinema seems to think anything is amiss. Back at the trattoria, the Frenchman and I raise the question of whether the Italian dub-meisters should have had the dubbing actor say, "Don't you understand Italian?" Much argument about the merits of each case; the Frenchman, a Jewish boy from New York, and I arguing that linguistic verisimilitude (or some such) required the use of "Italian", the others, a majority, argued that the audience (a) knew that the film was dubbed, and (b) everybody knew that English was really the language of the Wild West. So what's the problem? We appealed, in our limited but improving Italian, to the owner of the restaurant for his opinion, who in turn canvassed all his Italian patrons for their opinions. A big hubbub ensued, in the way that Italians are masters at, with opinions, gestures and arguments flying to and forth. *Il patrone*, entranced with the high intellectual quality of his restaurant clientele, offered our table *digestivi* (Marsala) on the house to keep the ball rolling. I can't quite remember how the discussion evolved, but I suspect that the Italians, long accustomed to having their foreign films dubbed rather than sub-titled, sided with the majority who would argue, when faced with such a linguistic incongruity, for the dominance of historical accuracy. For me, the evening was notable for the opportunity it gave me to try and argue in Italian, rather than handle service encounters or make inane conversation. As to the issue, I am to this day unsure as to the more appropriate response.

11

Close of play on my schooldays

So at eighteen, I am ready for university. As they say in cricket, stumps have been drawn on my days as a school-boy. I do not intend to dwell again here on the educational lessons that might have been gleaned from the foregoing accounts of educational incidents in my life so far. After all, this is not a didactic treatise. Rather, I will conclude by saying that I have emerged from my schooldays in many ways a success. (I learnt only 40 years later that my younger sister and still younger brother used to refer to me as "golden boy".) I was, as it happened, somewhat pretentious, a persona not helped by the posh accent that my privileged schooling and background had provided. However, I was aware how fragile my achievements were; I would never never have got a scholarship in history to Cambridge without the brilliant tutelage of Roger Lockyer. (Indeed I think I am right in saying that Lancing College had obtained almost no Oxbridge scholarships in history in the years preceding his arrival.) Yet another sign of a lucky star that illuminates this first chapter of this memoir (of sorts).

It took me years to rid myself of the pseudo-intellectual pretentious aura that surrounded me. And it may surprise people who know me now as to how shy and embarrassed I tended to be. I remember occasions on holiday with my parents when I would blush just because a young woman had entered the room. Indeed, since my early days in the hospital bed in Hastings, I had never had a female confidante. This would turn out to be a severe downside to my all-boys educational experience, and one destined to largely continue in my undergraduate days and beyond.

Unlike Evelyn Waugh, the school's most famous alumnus, my

memories of Lancing College are highly favorable. I did well at school, enjoyed the camaraderie of my friends, one of whom I am still in contact with, and had some excellent teachers, none more so than Roger Lockyer, who transformed my life. But I have never been back, principally due to the treatment at Lancing of my younger brother (some eight years younger). He went to the same local prep school as me and, like me, entered Lansing College in a lowly class. Thinking he might be a late developer as I had been, I believe they pushed him along faster and further than might have been appropriate (despite his considerable intelligence). In any case, at 16 he was discovered drunk in the buffet bar of Brighton railway station wearing his school tie. This last detail seemed enough for a new headmaster to expel him, my own headmaster having been elevated (quite rightly) to the vice-chancellorship of a small south-western university. My brother never really recovered from this setback and never successfully completed his secondary education. As I write this memoir, I sometimes think of making a return visit, perhaps to give some lecture to the sixth form on a linguistic topic, but my memory of my younger brother's harsh treatment has so far prevented me from doing so.

So ends Chapter One and my school days are over; in Chapter Two, I deal with my next six years where the story is more conflicted and less obviously marked by success.

TWO

Three Years at Cambridge and Three Years in Europe

12

The end of history

For my first term and a bit at university I was a history major. One emerging problem with this choice though was that I found myself reading the same books as I had in my final years at school, such as *Tanner's Constitutional Documents*. Another was that the first-year history students were a large class (some 200–300) and the lecturers to these large classes were—despite their considerable scholarly reputations—for the most part rather ponderous and stolid in their deliveries. Third, I did not get on well with the weekly tutor I had been assigned. He was a graduate student with a stammer who lived in a damp, gloomy basement. The Cambridge system, at least at that time, was for an individual hourly meeting with the tutor, where we would discuss the essay that the student had written. This essay might have been handed in a day or so earlier, or might be first read aloud by the student. For our sixth meeting or so, I had gone to the main university library and found some fairly obscure stuff on my given topic, something to do with peasant life in mediaeval France. As a result, for the first time in life, I had included some footnotes in my essay because this esoteric practice, I had noted, was what many real historians did. So I was reading aloud my essay, and then had to say, "There's a footnote here and this is what it says". At which my tutor stopped me and expostulated, "Swales, as a first-year student of history, you shouldn't be indulging in footnotes. It's just pretentious at this stage". I was more upset by this attack on my *amour propre* than I let on, and resolved to explore possibilities other than history. In the end, I now reflect, it was as much as anything the contrast between Roger Lockyer's tutorials and those I was now experiencing that impelled me to look elsewhere. So, a little later, I had a chance meeting at dinner at Queens' College with a student I didn't yet know who told me he was reading Moral Sciences. The student explained that this was what most universities called philosophy, that there were only about 20 students a year, that you were expected to think rather than read, that most people's favorite was Wittgenstein, who had died just a few years previously as a professor of philosophy at the university, and there was a Moral Sciences Club, where one evening a week you could hear famous philosophers give papers and hear philosophical arguments. I was hooked.

Looking back, I think the individual tutorial system as I experienced it was largely a waste of time for both parties, and this despite being occasionally offered a small glass of sherry. Indeed, it was only in my third and final year that I learnt to enjoy and anticipate these weekly encounters. As happened later, it would have been better—and much less a waste of money—to join up three or four students (especially in the first two years) so that we could better share and compare what we had been thinking. As a history or philosophy student, I was typically cast as the examinee or interviewee without much opportunity for extensive dialogic exchanges. Talking later to friends and acquaintances who had taken degrees at about that time at other universities, I concluded that Cambridge's antique system was too much of a hit or miss affair. Frankly this wasn't good enough in a university where lectures were not compulsory, where there was no continuous assessment of any kind, and where everything depended on the final examinations that took place only once a year in early summer. The system, such as it was, depended on recruiting bright young men (and much fewer young women) and allowing them to basically educate themselves by wide reading and by participating in the numerous cultural events that Cambridge had to offer. Many years later, I read an article by a senior British academic in which he argued that universities should be measured by what they had contributed in terms of "value added" to undergraduates between entry and exit. This was, in effect, "How far had they come from where they started?" Since Cambridge and Oxford undergraduates had typically started further along than entering students elsewhere, I doubt if my alma mater would have fared well under the "value added" criterion.

13

Not a philosopher either

My eighteen-month experience as a moral scientist was both interesting and challenging. My tutor, Peter Long, came from the famous King's College next door because my college did not possess a philosophy tutor. He was an interesting man, probably of lower-class background, probably an assistant lecturer, and with a very interesting face. (My attempts to call certain men "handsome" have been almost universally derided by women.) One of his main interests was in statements of the kind "It is raining or it is not raining" or "nothing can be red or green all over". These were assumed to be so-called analytical propositions that were logically true. Peter Long, and here at 50 years' distance I recognize that I am skating on thin ice, argued *au contraire* that the first proposition should be understood as "It is raining or it is snowing, or it is sleeting, or it is cloudy, or it is sunny, etc". In my second and final year of philosophy, Peter Long gave a talk at the Moral Sciences Club on this topic and was subjected to much harsh criticism, I suspect because it was seen as an attack on the great Immanuel Kant's discussion of analytic statements. Seeing my chain-smoking tutor coming under considerable intellectual duress, I felt emboldened to speak for the first and last time at the Club. I said something like, "Well, it is raining at spot x *and* it is not raining at spot y, even though spots x and y are very close". This was dismissed as a trivial empirical observation of no relevance to a philosophical discussion. Rightly, I suppose.

Unlike my experiences of the history lecturers, the philosophy ones were remarkably different. A. C. Ewing gave us a course that might have been called *Fundamental questions in philosophy*. This was well-prepared and highly coherent and, since I have been in the USA, I have since learned that it would here have been called "a survey course". For example, Ewing listed arguments for and against the various theories of truth. The course was pretty dry and almost without student involvement, but you could take very good notes. In contrast, there was a very young Canadian lecturer called Ian Hacking, who would later become one of the world's foremost philosophers of natural science. This was very high-powered stuff delivered as if he was always speaking to some famous philosophical society—enjoyable and impressive, but far above my head, and I suspect above most of those of the other auditors. The professor in the department was a certain John Wisdom (I kid you not). His lectures were fairly bizarre. He would lean his large bald cranium over the podium deep in thought for the first few minutes. (I sometimes thought he was trying to remember whether he had to buy milk as he bicycled home.) After this ostensibly pregnant silence, he would come out with some gnomic utterance, the one I best remember being "a pair of lovely black eyes". After this dramatic opening, he would proffer some other startling proposition such as "Other minds don't exist". He then searched his smallish class of twenty or so for one of the occasional visitors who had been attracted, by hearsay, to this eccentric event. And then said, "What do you think of that?" However, after these dramatic non-monologues, he retreated usually into standard expositions of philosophical argument. Perhaps even more bizarre was our lecturer in logic, Casimir Lewy, a member of a long line of famous Polish logicians. His course was, in contrast to Ewing and Hacking, certainly minimalist since he spent nearly all the time on three propositions that, as best I remember, consisted of "A vixen is a female fox", "A vixen is the name for a female fox", and "A vixen is defined as female fox". As best as I also recollect, this was all about entailment. Anyway, one exceptional day, a very bright student put his hand up unexpectedly and said something like, "I have read that Rudolf Carnap argues that . . . ". Lewy, who always looked rumpled and haggard, expressed some surprise that Carnap had argued any such thing and continued lecturing. At the beginning of the next class, Casimir Lewy appeared even more rumpled and even more haggard than usual and announced in his strong Polish accent, "Since the last lecture I haf read every vord Carnap has written and nefer did he say vhot you said he did". Needless to say, after this extreme due diligence, none of us ever raised his or her hand to make any other observations. We were as quiet as church mice.

I believe it is generally true that academics from the same discipline usually write in similar ways. There are exceptions that people can point to—in philosophy, for example, to Wittgenstein—but my experience would be that the proposition holds. Why then are lecturing styles so different? A. C. Ewing, dry and meticulous and rather like a local government civil servant: "Today, we will discuss three arguments for and three arguments against a coherence theory of truth". Lewy, with his complex analyses of three propositions, interspersed with simulated (?) giggles at the foolish claims of his opponents: "As for Strawson's views on entailment . . . " (hysterical giggles). So we never got to hear what Strawson's heretical opinions exactly were. And John Wisdom, with his gnomic utterances and his classroom culture of the bizarre. Are the differences due to personality? Or to some role model of a lecturer that had stayed with them since their student days? Or to certain educational beliefs about the purposes of lectures? Ewing, in his transmissions of accumulated philosophical thought, enabled excellent notes to be taken; Lewy, doubtless trying to sharpen our brains on the finer points of logic, left me with moderately useful notes. Wisdom, acting as some kind of guru on a mystical mountain top, provided me with nothing more than random scratchings. But of the three options I have outlined, I would still choose personality as the leading variable.

So, after two years at Cambridge I took the Part I examinations in

Moral Sciences and obtained a very ordinary Lower Second Class grade, sufficiently ordinary to have my scholarship taken away. Partly because of this I thought I had better move on from philosophy, but the main reason was a requirement to take a course in Mathematical Logic in my third and final year. This looked to be very hard for somebody who had not even reached the calculus stage in secondary school math. The one obvious escape route was into psychology, so that was the route I took.

14

Neither a psychologist

In order to move to psychology for my final year, it was necessary to take an extra summer term in the department. This was an eye-opening experience in a number of ways. One of the instructors was a charismatic gentleman called Richard Gregory, who would later become a well-known advocate for science and science education in the British national media. We were also lectured to by Donald Broadbent, the director of Cambridge's famed Applied Psychology Unit. We also heard indirectly about a disaster that had befallen one of the lecturers. At this time, experimental psychology was deeply into rats; in fact, whether the rat turned left or right at the end of the tunnel was supposed to tell us much about the nature of human learning. Well, this lecturer had been running a major series of rat experiments, and it turned out that what was causing the rats to make their decisions at the end of the tunnel was not the stimulus versus the control, but the fact that one arm of the tunnel had a slight breeze flowing through it, and it was this artifactual element that had been determining the animals' choices over the last many months. Years of work down the drain. I didn't really ponder this unfortunate story for a number of years, but when I started to do some research myself, it was a salutary reminder of how "the best laid plans" can so easily go wrong.

During this year, I had an excellent tutor, Dr Liam Hudson, who would later become professor of psychology at Edinburgh, and who would write, among other things, a well-known Pelican book called *Contrary Imaginations.* In this, he argued that the typical IQ tests did not investigate creativity and imagination, whereas something like, "Write down as many uses of a brick as you can think of" would investigate precisely those qualities. I used to cycle over to his house once a week where we would talk over, amongst other things, the present and future of psychology. On occasion, I would be asked to stay for a meal and then the discussion turned to other matters, such as recent cultural events in Cambridge. Toward the end of my final year, I worked hard on reading the psychology literature, but my hopes—and those of Liam Hudson—of obtaining an upper second were not realized. I got a lower second again; it looked as though I had lost my old skill of knocking off four good essays in a three-hour examination, even if one possible further factor was the fact that I overslept for the first exam and only arrived half way through. Anyway, it was clear that I had not done well enough to even think of a graduate career (perhaps in the U.S.) as a rat psychologist. Since the great Harold MacMillan had announced the end of compulsory military service, I wouldn't now have to go into the army for two years on graduation—to the pretended or real chagrin of my friends who had already done their military duty. Instead, I would have to get a job. My father wanted me to "do something in the city", doubtless in the hopes that I would eventually rise to the position of investment banker or some such. My thoughts, however, were somewhat more adventurous. One day, by chance, I saw an advertisement in the paper for five language *assistenti* to teach English in classical grammar schools in major northern Italian cities. Well, I did know a bit of Italian. I applied and was later interviewed by an Italian signora at the Italian Cultural Centre in London in late spring. At one point she asked me what I had studied at Perugia, and I replied "Etruscologia". "Etruscologia!" she exclaimed delightedly, and went on to say that she was an amateur etruscologist. So we talked about the famous well I had visited, and about the so-called Etruscan Arch in Perugia. That was that. I was in.

15

My three years at Cambridge

So what had I been doing during those three years up at Queens' College? Well, in addition to the lectures in my oscillating major, I attended a few lecture courses by Cambridge GLFs (God-like figures). One was F. R. Leavis's scurrilous course with some title like "The twelve worst poems by the twelve most famous poets". Naturally, this appealed to the large crowd of undergraduates who attended; it appealed doubtless to any anti-establishment tendencies we might have had, as we waited for the next barbed comment about the literary canon. The whole thing, in retrospect, was facetious, facile and fun. Of a very different character was Pevsner's course on English cathedrals. This was essentially a slide-show enlivened by a hugely scholarly and drily humorous commentary. He had an enormous wooden pointer to pick out architectural detail, and every time he wanted a new slide from the projectionist, he used to bang the butt-end loudly on the wooden floor of the podium. Another great performance, but of a very different kind.

I also did many of the usual things that male undergraduates of my time at Cambridge did. I played a bit of sport (squash and table tennis) and some cards (poker), went to pubs for pints of beer, and punted on the river. I also read prodigiously and fairly widely, because each of my three years, my room-mate was taking English. In my first year, I shared with William Dunlop, who later became an Associate Professor of English at the University of Washington in Seattle. He also was a poet and co-edited the well-known literary magazine *Granta* with Margaret Drabble, who wrote a very warm obituary for William when he died a few years ago. My second year, I shared with Richard Lindley, of whom more in a moment, and my last year, my room-mate was Waris Hussein, who later became a well-known television and film director. Waris had considerable dramatic flair and a very creative visual sense, and I learnt from him what I know about the appearance of things on the stage or screen.

But as much as anything, I went to the cinema. I joined the Cambridge Film Society, and in my final year I was secretary of the society while Richard was president. This involved the two of us traveling to London to pre-view films that we might want to show during the autumn and spring terms. The Association of British Film Societies, over a long week-end, booked a small cinema in London and showed the films available for pretty well 48 hours non-stop. Richard and I watched and slept through most of it. However, choosing the films was not an easy matter because the Cambridge Film Society consisted of two very different audiences; regular members of the town and gown who had over the years seen most of the best films ever made, and the undergraduate members, many of whom had seen very few of the classics. So, we had to juggle together a program with several classics (i.e. *Citizen Kane*) for the neophytes, but with some unexpected and unusual items to draw in the old hands. As I remember, we did this pretty well, except for what I recollect to be Grémillion's 1943 *Remorques*. There were lots of gloomy, foggy waterfront scenes as I remember; it was almost universally panned by the audience, despite the presence of a moody Jean Gabin in his ubiquitous raincoat. The noirish atmospherics apparently didn't counter the banality of the plot.

One of my jobs as secretary was to cycle down to the railway station on the day of the film society meeting to pick up the cans of film and take them to the projectionist. Next morning, I had to cycle them back and have them carried to London on the train. Richard, who later became a well-known journalist on the famous current-affairs program *Panorama*, had as president the task of making all the announcements. Richard did it with considerable elan, because like Waris, he was a regular on the amateur Cambridge stage. I remember Richard's lead role in my college's dramatic society's production of Auden's verse play "The Ascent of F6" and Waris' performance as Tom Thumb in Fielding's play of that name, including sailing around the stage on roller skates. The couple of times when Richard couldn't be there and I had to make the announcements, I was a nervous wreck.

16

Se Parigi avesse il mare, sarebbe un piccolo Bari
(IF PARIS HAD THE SEA, IT WOULD BE A LITTLE BARI)

When my appointment letter came from the Italian government, I wasn't after all going to go to one of the top *licei classici* in Florence, Rome, Milan, Bologna or Venice. My letter said that I was to be the English assistant at the Scuola Commerciale G. Gimma in Bari. I didn't even know where Bari was, and I had to search most of the way down the map of Italy to find it. Southern Italy in 1960 was thought to be very underdeveloped, to be rife with honor killings, and to be under the control of the Catholic church and the mafia. What had I let myself in for? In fact, my anxieties increased when I entered the province of Puglia. My grandfather had left me 500 pounds in his will, which in those days was just enough to buy a Morris Minor for export, without having to pay purchase tax. (In fact it was 499 for the car and one pound for affixing a GB plate on the back.) So somewhere in the vicinity of Foggia I got a bit lost, there being no expressways in that part of Italy at that time, and in some village a group of boys starting throwing stones at the car. (I was later told that the boys probably thought it was a German car.)

Bari turned out to be a crowded and bustling city, and I found a room near both the centre and the school. The principal was a very charismatic gentleman determined to make a success of this more modern type of secondary school, and his charismatic determination doubtless had something to do with the fact G. Gimma was one of only five schools in the country—and the only one in the south—to have the very uncertain advantage of employing an official "assistente inglese". My duties were to teach, along with two other Italian English teachers, commercial English to segregated classes of either girls or boys. The textbook material was somewhat old-fashioned since it contained sample letters that tended to begin with the likes of, "We are in receipt of your esteemed order of the 16th ult. and hereby confirm that we will ex-

ecute your order with all careful and expedited dispatch". We also had
to teach some commercial "life and institutions" material such as the
functions of the Bank of England, Lloyds and the stock market, as well
as which British cities produced what. As I remember, Leicester was
stockings and Northampton was shoes. There was also a decent grammar book written by a certain Professore Lanzisera. This helped me
with all the bits of English grammar that I hadn't a clue about, such as
the basic rules for article usage. It also had an excellent joke in it, which
went something as follows: A visitor arrives at Milan airport and takes
a taxi into the city center. As it passes a building under construction on
the outskirts, the visitor, an American engineer, asks when it will be finished. The driver replies "in about a year", to which the visitor comments, "Well, back in Texas, we would have that finished in six
months". Two similar exchanges take place as they approach the city
center—to the increasing annoyance of the taxi-driver. Finally, they
reach downtown where resides the splendid gothic cathedral of Milan.
The American points to it and inquires, "Say, what's that building over
there?" The taxi-driver turns, looks at him and replies in a deadpan
voice: "I don't know, Sir; it wasn't there yesterday". This joke, or rather
suitably localized variations of it, has always gone down a treat as the
close to short speeches at receptions, banquets and the like, especially
in lesser developed countries. I have used it on and off for 40 years.
Thank you, Prof. Lanzisera.

I learnt from my two colleagues, Maria and Franca, how to grade
student papers; in particular, this involved a bi-coloured pencil with
blue graphite in one half and red in the other. The blue was for minor
mistakes and the red for serious ones, and it took me some time to understand how the categorization should be applied. Maria was, I guess,
in her early forties and was married to the principal of a middle school,
but they had no children. Anyway, my room in the fourth-floor apartment in the same street as the school was becoming a bit awkward;
there was a shared bathroom and a small shared kitchen for the widow
who owned the apartment, a batchelor professor of demography at the
university, and a youngish married couple, as well as myself. It was decidedly cramped and it also soon turned out that the husband became

extremely jealous if either of us men indulged in even the most innocuous of conversations with his wife. I was explaining this to Maria one day when she said, "Why don't you come to live with us in the *periferia*? However, Maria went on to explain that some diplomatic preparations might be necessary since her husband Gino did not speak any English—worse, he had been captured by the British in North Africa during World War II and been a prisoner of war of the British for eighteen months or so, when he had lost a lot of weight because of the poor food. Anyway, after a bit Gino was persuaded to allow a Brit to occupy their spare bedroom (at first on an experimental basis), but I lived contentedly with Gino and Maria for the rest of my time in Bari. I provided some intellectual stimulus and made a valuable third at the card-table, especially for a demanding card game called *Scoppone Scientifico*. Perhaps in some small way I was also thought of as an adopted son. Gino himself was something of a local poet and was a splendid representative of that "Magna Grecia" southern Italian culture that had flourished in the first half of the 20th century, primarily under the tutelage of Benedetto Croce. Among other accomplishments, he could speak very passable Latin.

17

"Lettore" at the University of Bari

After I had been in Bari for a couple of months, a vacancy arose at the University for a native speaker of English to work 12 hours a week as "lettore" in the English department at the university. Since there were very few other native speakers in town, I got the job. The professor and head of department was—as was quite common in Italy at that time— essentially an absentee appointment. He spent most of his time at an Italian Institute in a northern European capital, coming to Bari to give a few lectures just before the exam period and to supervise the examinations. When I had a first meeting with him after my appointment, he explained that one of my main jobs would be to teach English conversation to the first and second years since I was the only native speaker they had on the staff. I inquired how many students there were in the first year class and he said, "nearly two hundred". I was so green about English language teaching that I didn't realize at the time that it might turn out to be problematic to teach conversation to 200 people sitting in a large lecture hall! So, undeterred I entered the class and announced that I was there to teach conversation. "No, no", they all shouted, "dictation, *dettato*". The reason for this insistence soon became clear. In order to cut down on his workload, the professor had introduced a system whereby the first-year students could not take any of the other English examinations until they had passed the dictation, and the dictations were so difficult that only about 20 out of the 200 managed to pass each time.

So, we consistently practiced dictations in preparation for the examination. One time, I remember, the Prof had chosen for the exam a fiendishly difficult passage from, if memory serves, some autobiographical work by Osbert Sitwell. The sentence that remains in my mind to this day was the following: "I wandered into the attic and what did I find but an assegai, a croquet hoop and a knobkerrie." This was patently unfair to a group of students, nearly all female, who had hardly ever left the south of Italy and had had little access to English-language books. So, it soon became an Us versus Him situation. In the examination room, I read the passage very slowly, three times, and with a strong Italian accent, rolling my r's like an operatic tenor so that they would have a better chance of "getting" words that ended in r or re. I graded as leniently as I could, but the prof checked my work and told me off for not scrutinizing the student answers carefully enough. After some further discussions, I think we managed in the end to allow about a quarter of the class to take the rest of the examinations.

The examination period was fraught in other ways. As always in Italy, many of the exams are oral, in which a student presents herself to an instructor to answer questions on, say, "English literature from Shakespeare to Shelley". Over the 20 minutes or so, the student can get questions about anybody and of any kind, so the whole thing is a bit of a crap-shoot and, consequently, gives rise to much anxiety. In addition, in the Bari of those days, it was a struggle for the students to get a suitable time-slot; for this they had to negotiate with the wizened and tiny senior clerk of the department, who controlled the examination schedules and for an underhand consideration of 500 lire would usually offer to be accommodating. Finally, I had to be careful in shops at examination time. As the only person with a grey Morris Minor in town—and the male inhabitants of the city were largely crazy about cars—I soon became easily identifiable. So, for example, in the stationery emporium, I might be purchasing some paper and ink, and the manager would come across and say, "Professore, for you a discount of 40 percent, and may I recommend my niece, Maria Manzoni, who is taking your second year class on Bacon's Essays?" (My favorite class by the way.) Another ethical dilemma—accept the discount but ignore the *racommandazione*, or go elsewhere?

18

Tutoring experiences

Apart from my two little jobs, officially totaling 30 hours of work a week, and which produced a monthly salary of 120,000 lire (about 60 pounds at the exchange rate of the time), I also did some private tutoring. This covered pretty well the gamut of Pugliese society in the early sixties. At one end, I gave private lessons to the two unmarried daughters of one of the leading professors of medicine, who (inevitably) also operated a large private clinic. Visits then to a splendid villa outside of town with servants offering me aperitifs of various kinds. Also, for a short time, I was enjoined to teach a little English to the richest young man in town, whose father owned the only large factory in the vicinity. This didn't work for long since he was often found to be elsewhere when our appointed lessons were due to take place. In one of our last meetings, he explained to me just one of his problems. When taking a signorina out for a meal in one of the splendid seafood restaurants down the coast, he was often conscious that the young woman's mother might have suggested to her to put sand or sugar in the petrol of his Maserati. This was because of the local custom that if a young man did not return a young woman to her family residence by mid-night, he would be required to marry her. So, with a sigh, he said that if he had any suspicions, he would organize an employee from his father's factory to follow behind in a back-up vehicle. I don't really know how valid his concerns were, but it made an interesting story.

At the other end of the spectrum was a male student trying to finish his thesis in order to obtain his five-year degree. The professor had assigned him to translate into Italian an obscure Jacobean play ("Secanus"?) and he had (understandably) been struggling with the English of his source text. The professor also found fault with the style of the Italian, but asked if I could help, at least with the former. I travelled two or three times to a very poor town in the nearby hills, where the family resided. The father was a *contadino* or peasant farmer, probably struggling to survive at the tail-end of the pernicious share-cropper/*mezzadria* system. In these circumstances, I didn't ask for anything for my attempts to improve the accuracy, if not the quality, of the translation. A couple of weeks later, the father turned up in the clerk's cubby-hole at the English department and left a sack for me. Inside was a live chicken as recompense for trying to help his son complete his degree. I took it cackling back to Maria and Gino, where I think we gave it to their part-time maid, Caterina. From Caterina, I learnt what I knew (but have now largely forgotten) of the Pugliese dialect. (Maria came from Veneto and could speak Venetian as well as standard Italian; Gino spoke traditional Italian with many subjunctives, most of which have now disappeared from normal speech.) Gino was a punctilious gentleman and was regular in his habits. One of Caterina's jobs was to look out of the window to watch for the *Preside* descending from the bus at the far end of the square at the close of the school day at about two o'clock. That was the signal to throw the pasta into the boiling water, and by the time, Gino had crossed the square, bought his daily newspaper from the kiosk and climbed the flight of stairs to the first-floor apartment, the pasta would be perfectly *al dente* and ready for serving.

In the middle of this socio-economic stratification were a group of English teachers, including Franca, one of the other English teachers from G. Gimma, who wanted me to help them prepare for the *abilitazione*, the official state exam that, if successfully passed, would guarantee a permanent position in the state educational system. I can't remember much of the details, but there were about five of us who used to meet in the evenings, including a single young man. One of the group was a shy and retiring young woman from a humble background. After several months, it was announced that the regional *abilitazione* competition for a limited number of permanent jobs would take place in Naples. To my horror and disgust, the family of the shy young woman said she shouldn't go because there was no male family member to accompany her and so "protect her honour". I went to their cramped apartment and expostulated in angry and I'm afraid less than fluent Italian, but to no avail. Later in the Arab world, I would have similar experiences of potentially upwardly mobile women being held back by family obstructionism of this kind.

Because I was a member of the university, various *assistenti* in other areas contacted me to help them with their English. One was Nico Perrone, who was working as a law assistant on a publication regarding the mineral/oil rights in the Red Sea. I helped him revise his paper, which was then sent off to a journal editor in Oxford. The editor was, to my great surprise, quite critical of the English revisions I had made. One I remember was his insistence that *suggest* should be followed by the subjunctive, as in *"This analysis suggests that the interpretation of the law* be *not dominated by powerful oil-company lawyers from Saudi Arabia"*. I had never noticed this and had always used the indicative, and I felt embarrassed that my writing style was shown to be limited in this way. Both Nico and his close friend Umberto Belviso (whom I also got to know well) would finish up as full professors at the University of Bari. Umberto became an expert in Italian commercial law and co-authored a good number of law textbooks and manuals in this field. Nico became a professor of history and, among his many publications, one of the most important was an investigation into the mysterious death of Enrico Matthei, the dynamic CEO of the Italian state oil corporation (ENI) in 1962.

We formed a group of left-wing intellectuals about town, staying, for example, to the end of Resnais' "Last year at Marienbad" while nearly all the rest of the audience had left in disgust at its inertness. Nico and Umberto also made me read the Marxist theorist, Lucaks, in Italian, but this turned out, as far as I was concerned, to be neither an easy nor a rewarding task. They introduced me to one of the Laterza brothers, the Laterza company being an excellent publishing house and bookshop in town. (Still going strong, I am glad to say.) It was arranged that I would write reader reports on scholarly books recently published in Britain with the aim of producing an opinion as to whether Laterza would commission an Italian translation. However, after a couple of trials, we mutually agreed to let the scheme lapse; I'm afraid that my formal Italian was not good enough, nor did I have sufficient understanding of the preferences of the Italian public.

A rather different group that I became entangled with consisted of three young men who were junior research assistants in nephrology. The senior of the trio, Sergio, knew no English but was due to speak at a conference at Oxford University on a research project carried out by the group and a professor of medicine. Could I help? I would go to their dingy office in the faculty of Medicine, where we would work on translating the paper into English and getting Sergio to read it out in a mostly comprehensible kind of way. They used to cook spaghetti for lunch in the lab every day, explaining that as *assistenti* they were too poor to eat out in even the humblest trattoria. Anyway, Sergio went to Oxford and stumbled through their joint paper on some aspect of kidney function. He said, however, that he couldn't really understand any of the questions, and the chair of this session in consequence had muttered to a colleague something like, "Where does this character come from?"

In retrospect, my approach to these teaching and tutoring activities was lackadaisical and cavalier. In effect, I just tried to wing it, relying almost entirely on the fact that I was an educated native speaker of the

English language. I didn't ask myself any questions as to whether I was teaching or telling, or whether I was creating plausible or useful kinds of educational interaction. I didn't read any books about how to teach English to foreigners, and I didn't do very much to sharpen my understanding of the structure of English, or to improve the way I explained how the rules of English grammar worked. In fact, I now believe that much of what I said was plain wrong. One particularly egregious example was the occasion in a university class when I believe I explained that English had five vowel sounds because it had five vowel letters!

19

An educational journey of sorts

I had to take my Morris Minor out of Italy every six months to avoid paying the heavy car taxes and to obtain when entering Italy again the cheap tourist petrol coupons, both activities being necessary on my small salary. After a couple of very long weekends driving from Bari to the Swiss border and back, late in 1961, I decided I would go to Greece on the ferry instead. So a few days before Christmas, Gunther, the *lettore* in German, and I set off for Brindisi, a couple of hours further south. When we got there, we discovered that the "ferry" at this time of year was actually a small Greek coastal trader called the *SS Miaoulis*. Half a dozen cars were lifted by crane up on deck and we set off. It became rough during the night and every time I went up on deck there would be the middle-aged German owner of a spanking new Mercedes with a bucket of fresh water and a rag. Between the waves that broke over the deck, he would rush out with his rag and try to wipe off the salt water that had sprayed on his pristine car. I believe he spent the entire night engaged in this Sisyphean task.

When we arrived at the island of Corfu, our intended destination, difficulties arose with the car because I had apparently failed to obtain the requisite tryptichs and carnets. (Where did they get these exotic names from?) Luckily, after we had explained that (a) we were just here for Christmas, and (b) it *was* Christmas, and (c) we would be staying only on the island, the customs officer allowed our car to be swung off the deck and onto the land, long after all the other cars had left. It transpired that the only hotel open was the grand Corfu Palace, which neither of us could even dream of affording, but we managed to find a couple of rooms in a house in the island's main town. The only restaurants open were two that catered to the local inhabitants, tourists apparently having abandoned Corfu as winter approached. In these, we were escorted into the kitchen to choose our dinner from a couple of bubbling pots, which usually turned out to be Goat Stew Number One and Goat Stew Number Two. One day, we started talking to an intelligent-looking man who owned a small antique shop. (Where I purchased a nice tulip-shaped wine glass, which Caterina soon broke back in Bari.) He turned out to be the local intellectual and used to tell us over an evening bottle how he knew the Durrells and had met Henry Miller and other expatriate Hellenophile literary lions. Gunther and I would later on those nights try to puzzle out how much of what our Corfu acquaintance said was true, how much rather unlikely, and how much obviously fanciful—an exercise that would on occasion prove useful in the future.

Christmas Eve found us resigned to a miserable dinner on the following day and walking along a deserted beach on the far side of the island, when a man emerged from a closed restaurant and asked if we would like to step through the back door into the kitchen and have a Greek (aka Turkish) coffee. In the ensuing halting conversation, he said he would open the restaurant especially for us for Christmas dinner since there would be little available in town. So on Christmas morning, we joined much of the local male populace at the local cinema for a series of short Charlie Chaplin films, and then in the afternoon, we dined in style overlooking the beach in an otherwise empty restaurant on roast chicken, roast rosemary potatoes and a green salad (all shredded into very small pieces as the Greeks strangely insist on doing). Verily, the kindness of strangers.

20

Extra-curricular activities and a first speaking engagement

A final group of acquaintances in Bari was a bunch of knock-about chums, with whom I would play cards or billiards, drink cheap Italian brandy and watch the girls go by. Two of these were brothers from a small town in Calabria, the younger (whom I knew better) was ostensibly a law student and the older ostensibly a student of architecture. I use the word *ostensibly* advisedly because I think neither had any real intention of completing their degrees and returning to their small home town. Their father had died when young, and all the remaining family members back home were female; the mother and sisters apparently received income from several orange groves that the family owned, much of which they sent to the brothers in Bari for the furtherance of their "education". Sario, the elder brother, was a particularly interesting case. In his apartment was an architectural drawing board, but the instruments on it had rusted solid from disuse over the years. Sario's student number was something like 400, while in 1962 entering students had numbers in six figures, thus indicating that he had first entered the university very soon after it re-opened following the end of the Second World War and had been there ever since. However, once a year his *dolce far niente* life changed; every year he was appointed chair of the committee which oversaw the student elections. These were always highly politicized, and largely a battle between the Communists and the Christian Democrats. Over the years, various and numerous attempts to rig these elections had been made. Sario had seen them all, and so for a few weeks each year he was really busy trying to minimize the amount of electoral fraud.

Towards the end of my two-year stay in Bari, I was asked by the small British-Italian association in the city to give a public evening lecture. Readers may be surprised to know that I chose to speak on 20th-century American poetry. The poems I chose to discuss were nicely printed on a couple of sheets; one poem I clearly remember choosing was Wallace Stevens' striking "Disillusionment of Ten O'clock" and where I think I talked about his repetitive variations on a theme and his symbolic use of colour. That poem ends this way:

> Only, here and there, an old sailor
> Drunk and asleep in his boots,
> Catches tigers
> In red weather.

I was nervous of course because this was my first public speaking arrangement. The smallish audience was, however, sufficiently kind about my performance. Except for Maria, who said to me afterwards something like, "Giovanni, when you speak in public take your hands out of your pockets, and don't scratch your head. Both are very distracting." Good advice, indeed.

I left Bari after two busy years, and only returned once—in 1994 while I was on sabbatical leave in England. To my surprise, I found Nico and Umberto still there, although now both professors at the university. I gave a talk in the English Department to the British *lettori* and *lettrici* and to my shock I found them to be (with one exception) as uninterested in and as uninformed about the craft of teaching English to foreigners as I had been. The only difference was that in 1961–1962 I was the single incompetent; now there were 20 of them.

I left Bari principally because I felt that I might be missing out on what appeared in Northern Europe to be "the swinging sixties". In hopes then of a rather different life-style, I applied for a job as a *lektor* with the British Centre in Sweden.

21

First hints of professionalism

My second job interview was somewhat different from the first, although it also took place in a smart area of central London. Of the interviewers, the key one was Anthony Abrahams, a barrister at Lincoln's Inn and co-director of the British Centre's operations in Sweden. Abrahams was a descendent of the famously athletic Abrahams who was the protagonist of that excellent film, *The Chariots of Fire.* I was quizzed about what I had read on English language teaching (virtually nothing), on how I would teach a class of Swedes who knew absolutely no English (vague remarks from me about using ostensive definitions (from my philosophy days) to give the names of objects in the room), and on how I had prepared the English teachers in Italy for their state exam (rather better). Anyway, I was accepted, though years later Anthony Abrahams, in one of those put-downs that barristers are noted for, at a lunch at the Director of the British Council's house in Kuala Lumpur, observed that the real reason why I had got the job was because "I had a nice smile".

I travelled to Paris that September to collect my faithful Morris Minor, which I couldn't take all the way to England because then I would have to pay 25 percent purchase tax. I had left it several weeks before outside a friend's apartment in the suburbs; it was now covered with leaves and had a flat battery. I then drove to Stockholm for a three-week teacher-training session, arriving the night before it was due to take place. I found a small hotel and parked my car in the street, only to discover next morning that thieves had broken into the boot and stolen all my LP records (mostly jazz), although thankfully leaving my books. I had lived two years in one of the supposedly most thief-ridden areas of southern Italy, but I had never experienced any events such as the one that occurred my first night in Sweden. So much for stereotypes.

The three-week training course was a real eye-opener; the main instructors were Ian Dunlop, co-owner of the British Centre in Sweden with Anthony Abrahams and the regular host on Swedish television's popular *Learn English* program, Michael Knight, and Dennis Gotobed, who unfortunately died at an early age. We were given much information about why many Swedes took evening classes in the winter months; we were taught some beginning Swedish by what I learnt to call the Direct Method (i.e. everything was conducted in Swedish), taught some very valuable methodology, and we prepared for and taught a couple of evening practice lessons. We were also introduced to the teaching materials that would sustain us later in our frozen outposts; these, as best I recall, were either situational-functional (i.e. useful phrases when on the telephone) or grammatical (exercises, for example, on the different uses of the verbs *say* and *tell*). We could order these from the head office in Stockholm a few days ahead of time and have copies sent to us in the provinces.

My designated patch consisted principally of the two nearby towns of Borlänge and Falun in west-central Sweden; additionally, I went to the nearby sawmill town of Hofors for classes on Friday evenings. I lived in a male hostel attached to the big steelworks in Borlänge, most of the other men being technicians from the company. In each of the three towns I had a "chaperone", who helped with putting adverts in the papers about my evening classes and with generally drumming up custom. I am guessing that I was given this posting partly because I had a car since there was a considerable amount of travelling involved. As I was supposed to give 28 50-minute lessons a week, I was pretty busy with travel, classes, ordering materials, preparing for classes and the like. I gave conversation classes for final year students at the grammar school in Falun and at the comprehensive in Borlänge; I visited every elementary school in the district to give sample lessons for the fifth grade; I had evening classes in all three of the towns; there were two morning housewives groups, and I was also supposed to run teacher-training workshops for groups of English teachers. Whew!

22

Across the frozen lakes

The winter of 1962–1963 was a particularly cold one in northern Europe, and this certainly included central Sweden. One day, I remember that the weather news on the radio forecast a minimum night-time temperature of −27 degrees C (about −20 degrees Fahrenheit); at this juncture, even the Swedish weather service admitted that it would be *mycket kallt* ("very cold"). So, on the mornings when I would be venturing afield to teach my two lessons to the elementary school in some hamlet or village, the directions from the school district office might go something like this, "When you get to the village of so-and-so, you can go either all way round the lake to the school at so-and-so, or you can drive directly across the frozen lake on the cleared track to the hamlet where the school is". Nothing ventured, I adopted the latter course without incident, except on the day when I finally met a car coming the other way along the snow-ploughed single track. We eventually managed to squeeze past each other, but neither of us could get our cars to move forward from a standing start on the slick ice. If he pushed car to get me going, he would then be stuck, and vice versa. "This is what we each do", he decided, "we get our engines running, engage second gear, get out, push behind, and then when the cars start to move, we run round, jump back in and drive off". It worked like a charm, and became a technique that proved useful on several later occasions. Decades later, when laughing at the Landrover-gate scene in that cult movie *The Gods Must Be Crazy*, I was reminded of this experience.

My visits to the elementary schools were a weekly highlight. The kids—probably fifth grade—were in their second year of learning English, and the underlying purpose of the visit was for them to meet a real English person and find out that they could understand him. Often when I arrived there would be a banner in English over the front door saying, "Welcome to our school" or some such. I used to give the same double-period lesson in each school, so by the end of the school year, I had it pretty well crafted. Much of it was concerned with polite requests of the "Would you like another glass of milk?", or, more ambitiously, "Would you like me to help you with that, teacher?" The lesson ended with a rehearsed simulated situation of a friend coming to tea— but with real cups and saucers, teapot etc—and engaging in the polite conversation we had been practicing. I usually chose a girl to be the hostess and a boy to be the visitor. (Well, I was pretty sexist in those days.) Sometimes, in the most rural schools, there would be only a dozen fifth graders, but in other places a full class. During my lessons, a number of teachers would sit or stand at the back of the room. The big moment came right at the end when I unexpectedly introduced another visitor to the tea party, a development which had not been rehearsed at all. I still remember the delighted expressions on the teachers' faces when a 12-year-old girl basically in the middle of nowhere managed creatively to say "Would *either of you* like another cup of tea?" In fact, there is a lump in my throat as I write about these incidents in an educational life that occurred 45 years ago.

23

A mix of teaching and learning experiences in Dalarna

My other teaching experiences were, as they say, somewhat variable. The Falun *läroverk* in those days was a very stiff and academic place with a long tradition. Indeed it celebrated its four-hundredth anniversary while I was there, and to the headmaster's annoyance, the German lector and I turned up late for the official ceremony. The members of the English department seemed to be obsessed with errors and their quantification. The Italians with their blue and red pencils had nothing on these guys, because (I believe at the instigation of the Ministry of Education and the crucial *Studentexamen* or School-leaving Certificate) here at the grammar school mistakes were assigned deductions ranging from −1 (very minor) to −10 (extremely serious). As soon as I came into the staff common-room, a voice from a corner grading English papers would inquire, "John, would you say 'I am here since January' is a minus six or a minus seven?" The effect of this heavy stress on accuracy had a severely deleterious effect on the fluency of the intelligent teenagers whom I saw once a week in order to practice their conversation skills. The wonderfully open and uninhibited children of the fifth grade had now become stilted and error-obsessed self-monitors of their (considerable) knowledge of English, and I had trouble liberating them from worrying about the mistakes they might make in Studentexamen English oral test.

On one occasion, the head of English had a formal dinner party to which I was invited. (I remembered to take some flowers for the hostess and also remembered to ask for an odd number of roses—a cultural requirement, at least at that time.) This was the one occasion in my year in Sweden when *titlerna* were used; that is, when talking to your neighbor at the dinner table, second person pronouns were dropped in favor of title plus last name, as in, "Would Mrs Svennson like some more potatoes?" Also the old convention was in force that only permitted drinking to take place when the hostess raised her glass to her lips—which always seemed to coincide with my having a mouthful of peas. The only other time I experienced this "titles" phenomenon was when I acted thirty years later as an oral examiner for a PhD thesis in Finland. The instructions were clear; the examinee was to be addressed by title, as in, "Would the honorable candidate like to explain why she had decided to focus on the discourse of forestry companies?"

An even more difficult teaching environment was the course I was supposed to give to the English teachers in the local area. In fact, this group knew English very well, had had some serious teacher education, and had considerably more teaching experience than I had. Frankly, I floundered, as I struggled to find obscure and useless bits of English grammar, or to offer dubious explanations of obscure idioms. The teachers were all very polite, but I am pretty sure nearly all felt it was largely a waste of time. Another group that turned out to be difficult was the housewives' group made up of the directors' and managers' wives from Stora Kopparberg, the mining company. In fact, they were a fluent, much-travelled and charming group of women largely, I guess, in their forties. The class rotated among their not inconsiderable houses, and from this simple fact emerged the problem. At the first morning meeting, we just were given orange juice to drink. At the next house the next week, it was coffee and cake; by about the sixth house, a lavish spread was being provided, consisting of open smoked salmon sandwiches, home-made canapés, and fruit salad. While it had soon become clear that my wives-of-executives group were using the English class as an excuse for social interactions (and there was nothing wrong with this in the Swedish provinces in the sixties), the competitive escalation in the food and drink being offered began to make everybody nervous. As a callow 23-year-old youth I didn't know to stop it, and I was relieved when the class came to an end.

The other housewives' group was much more fun; they all lived on the same unpretentious housing estate, and were planning to go together with their husbands and children to England for a holiday in the summer of 1963. They had agreed beforehand that nothing but coffee and *pepperkakar* (the ubiquitous Swedish ginger-snaps) would be served, that they wanted to learn vocabulary for homework, and wanted help with pronunciation. We did lots of situational stuff, like *At the Travel Agent's* and *At the Hotel.* I had fun acting the parts of rather slow-witted English employees who, inter alia, had great difficulty in spelling their names correctly.

Surprisingly, an even better experience was driving to the sawmill town of Hofors on Friday evenings for my beginners' class of local shopkeepers and the like. This took place, as best I recollect, from 5.30 to 7.30, and we had a break half way through. After a couple of weeks, the grocers and butchers and their wives used to prepare earlier that day a sandwich or two for me to eat—especially if I was driving after class to Stockholm for a week-end with other British Centre teachers. This became a huge game as they came up with fairly outlandish Swedish specialties, such as smoked horse sandwiches. They would gather round giggling to watch me consume elk entrail pâté or whatever it was, which I attempted to eat with true British *sang froid.* On one visit, my excellent Hofors chaperone introduced me to the local librarian who, it turned out, had completed a PhD in philosophy at Gothenburg University while earning a small living as a night-watchman in the port. We bonded quickly when I started talking about my experiences of philosophy at Cambridge. On several Friday nights, in consequence, I spent the night at his flat, where he and his charming Austrian wife entertained me with good food, drink and conversation. He had, during his studies, been to Oxford for some advanced short summer course in philosophy where one of the guest speakers had been the famous Oxford philosopher Gilbert Ryle. He recounted that at the end of the day Gilbert Ryle and some of the participants including himself had had recourse to the pub nearest Ryle's college, where Gilbert had gone up to the bar and ordered "a Ryle of bitter"—apparently a special measure somewhere between a half and full pint. Hofors Friday nights became an important event for me, given that I had failed to establish acquaintances with similar interests to mine in the other two towns. I regretted that we did not keep in touch.

24

Systembolaget woes

Then and now, the Swedish government runs the alcohol outlets in the country, the official off-licenses carrying the name of Systembolaget. At the time I was there, my local emporium in Borlänge was trying to persuade its customers to drink wine rather than spirits, and indeed large amounts of imported red wine were available from my old Italian province of Puglia, a welcome connection to my previous life. The Systembolaget's strategy was based on the well-founded belief that most Swedes, in their predominantly Lutheran country, were easily embarrassed in their off-license visits. In canny consequence, the liquor authorities had cut red linoleum footprints into the beige floor leading to the wine counter, so that customers, heads-down and shuffling forward in the queue with their disguising shopping bags, would be steered toward the grape rather than the grain or the potato. As far as I could see, this worked at least part of the time. However, the major socio-educational lesson I quickly learnt from the Systembolaget was that it was a total no-no to recognize anybody I knew in a building with such an unsavoury reputation. My early efforts along the lines of "Good evening, Mr Svensson, how are things going, and see you in class on Wednesday, and is there a red wine you would recommend?" were met with furtive avoidance behavior. I soon learnt that this was an incognito environment for everybody.

Given the very doubtful social status of official alcohol system, it is not altogether surprising that some of its employees were sufficiently ticked off by the way they were disregarded—if not despised—by the general public to go on strike in the spring of 1963. After they had been on strike for two weeks, there was nothing left on the shelves but a lone bottle of Stone's Ginger Wine. At my apartment block, there was a crisis meeting, and it was decided that the fastest driver and the fastest car, plus a couple of others, could make a lightening trip over the mountains to Norway to garner supplies. Our chosen leader was a technician with a Porsche who had taken a winter driving course with the famous Swedish rally driver of that era, På Taget (On the roof) Carlsson, and two others volunteered to go with him in order to bring back more bottles. On the appointed Saturday morning, they set off for Norway, in part supplied by me with smoked horse sandwiches from Hofors, willingly donated after I had explained the situation. Late that night, they wearily returned with several bottles to Borlänge and to an immediate great party.

For reasons that are still not very clear, I didn't renew my contract in Sweden, especially as this was the only job that I have had that didn't extend beyond a single year. Although the British Centre gave terrific support in terms of teaching materials and other advice, the 800 Swedish crowns a month that they paid was only marginally over a living wage. More importantly perhaps, the Dalarna I knew in the early 1960s was largely bereft of young men and women with my kind of interests and my kind of education; they had all migrated to the big cities. This was particularly the case with single young women; my remaining options for dates seemed to be teenagers from the high schools or secretaries in their thirties. If I had fallen in love, and I was perfectly prepared to do so, I might well have stayed—perhaps forever. Another factor that played some small part was that in the spring of 1963 the well-known historian Geoffrey Barraclough had given a lecture in Falun, sponsored by the British Council in Stockholm. I had a chance to talk to him afterwards at the inevitable coffee and pepperkakar, and began to think that I might be happier in a university environment. But I think the real reason for leaving was that I found myself at the bottom of the food-chain; I was dependent on the Centre's Stockholm office for nearly all inputs. Although I subsequently learnt from friends who stayed on that you could, after a further year or two, move up to materials writers or regional co-ordinators, I decided to look elsewhere for something more challenging. After three years in Europe, I was beginning at last to understand what might be done in my classrooms with the materials that I had ordered, or I had constructed myself largely from the simple fact that I was an educated speaker of the English language. However, outside the hermetically sealed world of my own classroom, I was largely uninformed and unthinking; it was, I thought, a time for new challenges, which constitute the next chapter.

THREE

Two Spells in Libya with a Post-Graduate Interlude

25

Entering the Orient

At the end of the last chapter, I intimated my feeling that I might be happier in a university environment, so on returning to the UK, I applied for lecturing jobs at the British Council, which acted at that time as a recruiting agency for many overseas universities. I applied for a lectureship in English at the famous Charles University in Prague, which naturally enough I didn't get. I also put in for one of three assistant lectureships in English at the University of Libya in Benghazi, the provincial capital of the eastern part of country, known as Cyrenaica. Somewhat to my surprise (my "nice smile"?), I was successful, again collected my Morris Minor in St Germaine de Près and drove to Naples. There, we (my car and I) embarked on a small Italian ferry for a leisurely four-day journey to Benghazi, with lengthy stops at Catania in Sicily and at Valletta in Malta. On the journey, I am afraid I appeared as stand-offish to a number of the British passengers because of my chattering away in Italian with the crew and my probably ostentatious study of a grammar of *Modern Standard Arabic*, replete with exercise examples of the following type: "Translate into Arabic, 'The princess has two beautiful brown eyes'".

On arrival, on a hot and dusty afternoon in September, 1963, I had some considerable delay in passing through Libyan Customs. After my car was eventually lifted off, I was assigned to a plump female Palestinian Customs Officer, who insisted that I unload all my books from the boot so that she could check them one by one against some Index of Forbidden Works. She spent a particularly long time on my copy of Faulkner's *The Sound and the Fury*, by now suspiciously battered, presumably because the title might be taken to invoking some type of revolutionary militancy in the relatively peaceful Libyan realm of King Idris. This was my first taste of that Arab suspicion of published words. Another came shortly later.

After getting established in a small flat rented by the university near the traditional market or *souk*, and finding my way around the Department of English and the College of Economics and Commerce, in both of which I was assigned to teach, I took advantage of the small university library to read up as much as I could about Libya. The university at that time was very young and, apart from the senior administrators, nearly all the staff were expatriates, many from the Arab World, but also including Nigerians and at least one tall, imposing Turk with a *tarboosh*. The best recent Libyan graduates were "demonstrators", anxiously working on their applications for graduate school, mostly in the U.S. Obviously, this was a group that I got to know quite well since we were similar in age and educational experience. Anyway, one of the books that I got to read about Benghazi was a surprisingly sexy novel by, if I remember, a Glyn Williams, the inaugural head of the English Department. When I mentioned to a bunch of these demonstrators that I had been reading this novel, to a man they turned on me and said that this was a bad book because the author asserted that there were black prostitutes in Benghazi who had come up from the southern oases. When I countered that this was a novel and that certain kinds of authorial license might be permitted, they responded that the book should be banned because there was no prostitution in Libya *tout court*. However, there were firm rumours that at least one such lady of the night plied her trade just a couple of streets from me in the "Arab Quarter". Much as I admire many aspects of Arab intellectual culture, I have never really come to terms with this disjunct between rhetoric and reality, the belief that you can say and write things that you know aren't really true, or deny things that are said or written that you know are really true. It is an odd kind of verbalism that never sat well with my empiricist upbringing.

26

A rich mix of English Department colleagues

One of my new departmental friends in Libya was an elderly gentleman called Dr Fred Koerner. Eventually, he revealed to me his background and how he had arrived at the University of Libya. It turned out that he had spent many years as horse veterinarian for the British army in Egypt (hence his doctorate). After being expelled following the Suez debacle, he had drifted westward along the North African coast until he arrived at Benghazi and its fledgling university college. He announced himself as an English speaker and as a doctor and was immediately hired as a lecturer in English language and literature. He lived in a room in a small Italian hotel in one of the main squares—and eventually died there—and was always happy to be joined at dinner by a young bachelor such as myself. At this distance, it seems that his teaching duties were light, largely consisting of introducing the more senior undergraduates in the English Department to the glories of Shakespeare. His favourite was *Twelfth Night*, although I doubt he ever got much past Act I, given the difficulty of this text for the students. Anyway, when walking around town, on occasion a young woman enveloped in the all-encompassing *barracan* would sidle up and whisper, "Mister John, if music be the food of love, play on". I immediately knew it was one of Fred's students (or former students) because he always made them learn the opening speech—as for such feats of memorization, they had of course an amazing facility.

The "Prof" of English was, in fact, a serious literature critic who had written—and would continue to write—a number of volumes devoted to key figures in British literature. He was also a serious musician with a clavicord in his villa and with a wonderful capacity to play the recorder in such a way that it seemed a serious classical instrument. (Indeed, when I was given permission to return home in 1964 for a couple of weeks because my mother was ill, he gave me firm instructions to go to Boosey & Hawkes, the famous classical music emporium in London, and purchase for him a couple of replacement strings for his clavicord.) He was also a canny Yorkshireman and fairly tight with his money. When his latest literary volume came out shortly before I left, it was dedicated "To my Teacher, Frank". While readers might think that this "Frank" was some God-like Oxbridge literary figure, he actually turned out to be the sergeant from the local British army base who had taught him to drive a car. Apparently, the canny Prof had not paid his driving instructor any money for the lessons, but seduced the sergeant into his *pro bono* activities with the promise of the dedication in his forthcoming book.

Another example of his canniness was related to me by Pablo Foster, one of the other assistant lecturers. Several members of the Department had decided to drive to Sebha in the southern Fezzan down the newly completed road into the Sahara. Some way down this wasteland, the four cars had parked by the side of the road for a picnic. A rare vehicle came the other way, stopped and announced that there was only one room available in Sebha's only hotel. At which, the Prof abandoned the picnic and the other travellers and hared off down the road to secure the room for his wife and himself. But the most intriguing example of his mindset was his apparently lifelong determination to secure academic positions which involved very little teaching. His classes had been boycotted at the University of Athens for a number of years because of the Cyprus troubles; he anticipated student strikes and university closure in Benghazi; he went to the American University in Beirut for much of the civil war; and, I believe, finished up at a brand-new Australian university at which no actual students were expected for at least two years.

Pablo Foster (so-called because he could draw well) was already in

Benghazi when I arrived, and the third new appointment was John Mann. The Prof said, with perhaps a twinkle in his eye, that he had only approved his appointment because he had played the Bach trumpet in the National Youth Orchestra. He dispatched Pablo and me to the local airport to meet him with strict instructions to "Send him on to Nairobi if he hasn't got his trumpet with him". So we met him coming down the aeroplane steps (yes, you could do that in those days) with our first and doubtless unexpected question, "Have you got your trumpet?" John M. said, "No, it's coming by sea, but I do have the mouthpiece to keep in practice with". Good enough we thought.

In later years, Pablo would become involved in writing new secondary school ESL textbooks for Tunisia, and then work in Scotland on adult literacy programmes. John Mann later became an English Language Officer with the British Council. John, in fact, had recently completed a post-graduate qualification in ESL at London, where he had become involved in some way with updating Michael West's *General Service List of English Words* published in 1953. I became intrigued by this volume because it showed you (in percentages) the more and less common meanings and uses of common words. For example, the entry for the word *post* shows that 49 percent of the 450 instances were used in its "mail" sense, followed by 26 percent in its sense of "position" or "job", and only 5 percent in its "lamp-post" meaning. These kinds of findings struck me as being more scientific than anything else I had come across in teaching English to foreigners, and probably kick-started what would become a life-long interest in the milder forms of the quantification of the English language.

My colleagues in the Faculty of Economics and Commerce were Americans, and the one I knew best was Bill Frazier, who had in fact a master's degree in ESL from the University of Michigan, although the significance of this did not register with me at all at that time. The American team leader was Dave Wigglesworth, and it was Dave who pushed the standard U.S. line of the time that learning a foreign language was almost entirely a matter of regular repetition and pattern practice so that appropriate and correct FL (foreign language) habits would be formed. This was, of course, an extension to language teaching of Skinnerian behaviourism in psychology, but, despite its attractive simplicity, I was never convinced that cognitive involvement and experimentation played no part in FL acquisition. Bill Frazier was also an Arabist and it was Bill I assisted on my first small materials development project. Bill wanted to produce a mimeographed English-Arabic dictionary of the common technical words in the students' Economics and Commerce textbooks. Since I regularly taught one of these (a Pelican paperback introduction to economics) to the second-year students as part of our fledgling EBE (English for Business & Economics) curriculum, I helped somewhat in selecting the English words and phrases to be targeted. In these various ways, I was beginning to become more interested in the field.

27

Embarrassing moments in the classroom

In a long teaching career, there have of course been many of these, often involving words in English that have a double meaning in the local language. Stuff involving birds and sausages in Italy, or *double entendre* requests by precocious female Swedish teenagers, such as, "Will you come in?" Or, on my first teaching visit to America in the late seventies, embarrassment caused by an off-the-cuff class comment that the inhabitants of Oregon would doubtless spend time "eating beaver". The most memorable of these, however, occurred during my first months of teaching Economics English in Benghazi, when I was going through a passage from the Pelican textbook I mentioned in the previous episode. I could tell something was coming up because of that anticipatory *frisson* that seemed to be transfixing the class. So, when the moment arrived, one of the students raised his hand with a barely suppressed grin and asked, "What's a zip, sir?" since the passage under explication used some example about a zip manufacturer. Always believing that ostensive definitions are best, I proceeded to open the fly of my trousers and pointed, saying, "that is a zip". Collapse of class into helpless laughter that I totally failed to understand.

After class I sought out Bill Frazier and asked him about the incident. After he in turn stopped laughing, he offered something like the following, "Well, John, as you know, Arabs have difficulty in distinguishing the sounds /b/ and /p/ because the difference is not phonemic in Arabic, and, as you probably also know, Arabic short vowels are somewhat variable, but what you obviously don't know is that in colloquial Arabic, the word for penis is *zob*, so what you were doing when you were pointing to your *zip*. Do I need to go on?" On the whole, a rather uncomfortable way of learning useful Arabic vocabulary.

28

*A teacher-training course in the capital city
and a school-leaving exam*

In the spring of 1964, we had a visit from David Wilkins, the dynamic young English Language Officer from the British Council in Tripoli. Several years later, David would become well known for developing the concept of a Notional Syllabus, structured around functions like "making excuses" or "giving compliments", rather than grammatical categories such as the present perfect tense, or phrase book–like situational ones such as At the Bank or Going through Customs. In fact, later David would become Professor of Applied Linguistics at the University of Reading. Anyway, David wanted to offer, under the auspices of the Ministry of Education, a summer in-service training course for a group of Libyan secondary school teachers of English. So, during the summer heat, Dave Wigglesworth and I made the two-day journey around the Gulf of Sirte to Tripoli in my trusty Morris Minor. We spent several days preparing materials prior to the course opening. At the welcoming event, a group of about 20 teachers turned up along with the Chief Inspector of English. However, the teachers made it clear that they wouldn't attend the course until they had received an allowance for the extra expenses involved in traveling to and living in the capital. The stand-off dragged on for days, to the growing irritation and frustration of the small group of assembled teaching staff. "Why couldn't they appreciate the opportunities for increased professional competence and career advancement this course would provide?" we expostulated. Eventually, the course got underway, but, if memory serves, it never really recovered from its much-delayed start. Looking back, I now have a greater appreciation of the teachers' dilemma. After all, they were relatively low-level civil servants on relatively low salaries from the smaller towns in the western part of the country. They had been selected to attend, rather than having offered to do so on a volunteer basis. They were away from their families, since most were married. And perhaps most significantly, they probably thought that if they didn't get their money for extra expenses up front, they would probably never get it. In effect, there was a clash of cultures here, and the well-educated Westerners' disdain for their "poor attitude" to the intellectual excitements being offered to them was, I later came to realize, misplaced.

At about this time, Pablo Foster was one of the team of examiners for the English language paper in the Libyan School-leaving Certificate, the *thanawiyya*. The most testing part of the exam was the composition essay. As it happened, available in the market were a series of booklets produced in Egypt offering advice on and practice in how to write English essays. Among other things, they used to offer suggestions for opening sentences, one being, *Nothing is so important in our daily life as _____*. Students were then advised to fill the blank with the topic of the essay. Unfortunately, the essay topic for the 1963–1964 year was "Space Travel". So, as Pablo related, the British Chief Examiner was all for failing every student who had been inattentive enough to open his or her essay with, *Nothing is so important in our daily life as space travel*. In the ensuing discussion, led largely by the Libyan and Egyptian members, a more tolerant attitude eventually emerged, and students would not be so harshly penalized for their inappropriate "daily life" opening. So, another clash of cultures.

29

Euesperides

Bob and Mavis Bond were contract schoolteachers with the Benghazi secondary schools, and I was the regular baby-sitter for their young daughter. One day Bob showed me a pile of highly corroded ancient bronze coins he had collected when walking his dog on a salt-marsh on the outskirts of the city. This location was the by-now-devastated site of Euesperides, the original Greek settlement. I also started to go there to look for coins, sherds, loom weights and bronze arrowheads, especially after heavy rains. Some months later, I was invited to a dinner where also present was Richard Goodchild, the brilliant Director of Antiquities for Cyrenaica, making one of his rare visits to the city from his up-country headquarters in Cyrene. I mentioned our finds to him, and he greatly encouraged me to try and clean them up, relate them to the British Museum Catalogue (the BMC) of ancient Cyrenaican coins that he would lend me, and prepare a draft manuscript for the impressive archeological journal *Libya Antiqua*, which was published in Rome. This I proceeded to do, especially as I thought it would do something to revive my low spirits following a busted love affair. The coins were frankly hard to clean; indeed, on one occasion I resorted to a bottle of nitric acid obtained from the local chemist. However, Bob and I eventually managed to make something out from 137 coins out of a total of about 200. I then spread these out on my dining room table, on small pieces of paper containing notations about weight, diameter, any symbols or legends and likely BMC number. With growing excitement, it slowly became clear that the sequence of coins might provide evidence as to when the salt-marsh city site was abandoned in the third century BCE for one closer to the sea. (Readers may care to know that the history of Cyrenaica at that time is uncertain and disputed, especially during the period known as "Magas in revolt".)

As I have already commented on the introductory paragraphs of the *Libya Antiqua* article in my *Other Floors, Other Voices* volume, here I will offer two short passages from the body of the paper. The first extract deals directly with part of the coinage:

> The Jerboa-Crab quarters (BMC 285 c-d), of which as many as five have been found at Euesperides, have been classified as belonging to the second Cyrene period, but only with reservations. All the examples so far published lack lettering of any sort. The coins are also smaller and thicker than the usual quarters of this period and carry a quite pronounced circular incuse. In fabric and type of corrosion they are very reminiscent of BMC regal coin 27 (EU 124-7). The crab reverse and unusual appearance of these coins again raises the possibility of an autonomous mint at Apollonia, the existence of which remains controversial.

At 45 years distance, this kind of writing now strikes me as remarkably professional and competent, especially as Richard Goodchild only made a series of minor corrections when I submitted the manuscript to him. Indeed, the article contains vocabulary that escapes me now—not only *incuse* from the above extract but also the likes of *Hippodamian*, *exergual* and *mericarp*. The second extract deals with the interpretation of the data:

> The numismatic evidence implies that the transfer to the promontory site had taken place some time before it received the name of Berenice from Euergetes I; it may even be the case that the Euesperides had already been abandoned by the date of Berenice's accession. Of course, the fact that a new name was given to the city does not necessarily mean that the city was refounded at the same time, for contemporaneously with the renaming of Euesperides Tauchira received the title of Arsinoe and there is no evidence of a change of location at the latter city. Further R. G. Goodchild (*Benghazi— the story of a city*) refers to a statement by Solinus to the effect that Berenice not only gave her name to the new city, but also "fortified it". This suggests that there was some settlement to fortify.

Again, I would suggest to the reader that the argumentation here is quite impressive from an archeological viewpoint. Indeed, I may have been getting ahead of myself—and I use *myself* for I did all of the writing. At one point, I had the temerity to claim that the curators of the British Museum might have misclassified one coin, proposing that "BMC 286 really belongs to the Regal coinage". Over the years this claim has been queried, and it has become clear that challenging the austere authority of the British Museum Catalogue is not something one can do with impunity. For example, a correspondent in 1980 wrote to say that I was wrong in this re-attribution, "The obverse types differ, so too the fabric as far as one can tell; and of course, the legends". The rashness of youth!

It might be thought that the 1965 article, R. C. Bond and J. M. Swales "Surface finds of coins from the city of Euesperides" would not continue to reverberate in the scholarly literature of early Libyan history. After all, it was written by a very temporary and very amateur numismatist in the mid-1960s. Not so. In a 1994 publication from Ted Buttrey, then at the Fitzwilliam Museum in Cambridge, but previously a professor at Michigan, again I am taken to task: "The published attribution of the single Soter/Libya piece (Bond and Swales 136) to Group I, is wrong". (Detailed reasoning follows.) Later, Buttrey does however offer some (qualified) approval:

> As to the state of the new city, Bond and Swales wrote of their finds, 'This numismatic evidence implies that the transfer to the promontory site had taken place some time before it received the name of Berenice from Euergetes'. I believe that the coins show their case for the pre-Euergetes transfer to be correct. But their assumption about the name of the new site is another matter. Actually Solinus only informs us that Berenice fortified the city, and that she was married to Ptolemy III. He does not connect these two facts. . . . Even accepting Laronde's argument that 'fortified' is equivalent to 'founded', nothing requires the conclusion that it was as Ptolemy's wife that Berenice (or those who exercised authority in her name) founded the city. On the contrary, . . .

One clear lesson I would draw from this important episode in my academic life is that enablement was provided not so much by Richard

Goodchild's support, but more by the confidence he expressed that I could do the analysis and the write-up. Although both aspects turned out to be very tough, I managed in the end, and to this day, I try to adopt a similarly exhortatory role when discussing research projects with students, junior colleagues or visiting scholars. The other lesson is that authorial credit is not something to become heavily exercised about. Bob had many more coins than me, so it seemed natural at that time that he became first author. After all, I was happy with the intellectual satisfactions of getting a job well enough done—apart from the grisly story of BMC 286. In fact, it was some time later that I came to the conclusion that the only way to be happy as an academic was to be generous with your stuff and to be generous with your fellow academics. By that time, I had seen too many lecturers succumbing to something close to paranoia because they believed (rightly or wrongly) that somebody had stolen their ideas or their data without due acknowledgement.

It might be thought that I might well have considered a career as an archeologist as a result of this first publication, especially as in 1965, I also spent some time helping out at an ancient site down the road from Benghazi, where John Hayes, whom I had known vaguely at Cambridge, was carrying out a small excavation. On Fridays, I used to bring him a few supermarket supplies and help with the attempted reassembly of broken pots, an activity which I now believe is called "sherding". But I don't think I ever seriously considered it. Instead, I wrote to Leeds University, applying for a place for the 1965–1966 year on its Diploma in ELT and Linguistics. They wrote back, suggesting I arrange to come up for an interview when I returned to the UK. But first, I had to leave Libya.

30

The final exit visa

One of the bits of business you had to do before being granted a final exit visa was to show that you had paid your electricity bill. It happened that I was the first occupant of the brand-new small block of flats that the university had leased for some of its academic staff; indeed, the plaster was hardly dry on the walls on my arrival. It also happened that the electricity was on when I moved in and I had never received a bill during my 20 months of residence. So, prior to departure, I go to the electricity office, where this conversation (or something very like it) takes place in a mixture of English, Italian and Arabic.

> *Me:* Good morning. I have come to pay my electricity bill. I live in Flat 1 in Building so-and-so on such and such street.
>
> *Clerk:* Let me try and find the file. (Long wait). I have found the file, but you have no electricity because you never paid the meter-connecting-up-charge.
>
> *Me:* Well, I do have electricity and I would like to pay my bill because I need your clearance to get a final exit visa.
>
> *Clerk:* I am afraid that is not possible because you have never paid your connecting-up charge, and therefore have no electricity.
>
> *Me:* In that case, perhaps you can give me the clearance that I owe you no money.
>
> *Clerk:* You work for the university, is that not so?
>
> *Me:* That is so.
>
> *Clerk:* It is probable then that you can read.
>
> *Me:* Yes, it is probable that I can read.
>
> *Clerk:* If you can read, it is probable that you want to read at night, and therefore it follows that you may have electricity. It is most irregular since you have not paid your connecting charge, but I will send a meter-reader with you to look at your meter.

(So, the meter-reader and I drive to my flat, where I find for the first time I have locked myself out. So I go to the upstairs flat, climb down the internal well in the building and let myself in through my open kitchen window. I open the front door, let the meter-reader inside, who proceeds to read the meter. We then return to the office.)

> *Clerk to meter-reader:* He has electricity?
>
> *Meter-reader:* Yes, he has electricity and the meter reads so-and-so. But there is a problem.

Clerk (a furtive smile crossing his face): There is a problem? What is the problem?

Meter-reader: It is not his flat. He doesn't have a key.

Me: Of course it is my flat; I just left my key inside. This is the first time it has happened to me in two years.

Clerk: Perhaps that is the case and perhaps not. I'm afraid you will have to get a letter from the university confirming that this is your flat before you can pay your bill and get your clearance.

(Exeunt)

31

Professor Terrence Mitchell

I had applied to Leeds principally because Terry Mitchell, the Professor of Linguistics at that university, had given a public lecture at the University of Libya some months before I left. He opened with a prepared speech in classical Arabic, which I couldn't follow but really impressed the Arabs in the audience. He then proceeded to describe some of the features of up-country colloquial Arabic based on transcripts he had constructed after conversations with elderly tribesmen when he had served as a British army intelligence officer in that area nearly twenty years previously. This was a demonstration of what a great field linguist could do—and of course at a time when the tape-recorder hadn't yet been invented. I remember the President of the university observing in the ensuing discussion that nobody spoke quite like that anymore, and that Professor Mitchell's readings aloud gave him an eerie sensation that his grandfather had come back to life. When a group of us went up to him afterwards at the podium, we noted that he had been reading aloud from what I subsequently learnt to call a "very narrow phonetic transcription".

In due course, I made my way to Leeds for my interview with Terry Mitchell. Early on in our conversation, he asked me if Benghazi bus-conductors were still referred to as *bigliettaui*, an Italian loan-word. I replied that I didn't know since, having a car, I had never been on a Benghazi bus. But I did manage to list some Benghazi names for car parts that were Italian loans, such as *candela* for spark-plug. He then asked me what I had read on the topic of linguistics and English language teaching, and I mentioned the recently published volume by Halliday, MacIntosh and Strevens. When I said I had been very impressed, he made a harrumphing noise, and changed the topic back to the Benghazi *souk*. After twenty minutes of interview (or thereabouts), he brought matters to a close by saying, "Well, Swales, you seem a nice enough chap; you will be welcome in early October". I was admitted to the Diploma A course (which was raised to a master's degree the following year); unlike the Diploma B course, the A was designed for people who had had a few years of ELT teaching experience. It hardly needs pointing out that, as the decades, have passed, the process of applying for a master's degree has become increasingly generified. For example, graduating seniors at the University of Michigan in 2009 have to produce a bundle of documents, such as a transcript of their undergraduate performance, a CV, a two-page "statement of purpose", an application form, and two or three letters of recommendation to get accepted on a master's course. No more just a short interview, with no preceding documentation except a short letter, and "you seem a nice enough chap"!

32

Courses at Leeds

There were about 25 of us enrolled on the Diploma A course, about 20 men and half-a-dozen women. Several of the men, mostly older than me, were English Language Officers with the British Council who had been seconded for a year's training. Nearly all of the full group had had experience teaching English overseas, which meant that tutorials were much enlivened by reflections on those experiences.

Professor Mitchell's course on general linguistics was full of intriguing detail, but did not offer a very successful overview of the field. (Rather like my own lectures, I might surmise.) Some of that detail, I recollect, involved an analysis of phrases like *hot-buttered toast, a hot-headed Irishman*, and *a hard-boiled egg*. He demonstrated that, despite their similarity in surface structure, there were important underlying differences, such as the initial adjective could be dropped in the first and third phrase, but not the second. Another tour de force was his discussion of adjective order in English based, surprisingly, on descriptions of antique furniture, as in "an attractive early 19th-century mahogany cross-banded breakfast table". Not, I think, at all for my personal benefit, he also talked about his 1957 study of the discourse of buying and selling in the Benghazi *souk*, which I, and others, would later consider to be a classic pioneering piece of oral discourse analysis.

As part of the Diploma, we were required to take short courses in English poetry and English fiction. The former was taught by the poet Geoffrey Hill and was consistently interesting. The fiction course was offered by a senior professor, whose name I will forbear to mention and who, on several occasions, had apparently stopped at the senior common room bar on the way over. One particularly excruciating hour was devoted to him telling us all the acronyms of all the English literature journals in the world. We could write our assignments on a topic of our choice from either poetry (to be marked by Geoffrey Hill) or on prose (to be marked by the other guy). Foolishly, I chose to write about my favourite novelist at the time, William Faulkner, and worked very hard on it, producing a long 30-page essay and even persuading my sister to type it up for me. Most of my fellow-students took this assignment much less seriously. It was only months later that I learnt that all those post-graduates who had opted for prose had been given the identical mark of 34 out of 50. Clearly, the anonymized professor hadn't bothered to read any of our work.

The star lecturer on the course was Michael Gregory, who taught us syntax and later migrated to the University of Toronto. He gave us, chain-smoking all the way, a dynamic and fast-paced introduction to a recent version of Halliday's grammar called "category-and-scale". After each of these 50-minute lectures, we were exhausted, trying to get down on paper his rapid-fire diagrams, examples and entertaining comments. He also was the first lecturer I had encountered who didn't hesitate—and perhaps rather relished—to introduce taboo words into his exposition; I remember some few minutes being devoted on one occasion to the syntax of the verb *fuck*. He was also very approachable, if somewhat intimidating, and would often join a group of students for coffee and further syntactic discussion after the lecture. We were also assigned tutorial groups to work further on syntax, and my tutor was a PhD student finishing his dissertation. On one assignment I criticized one aspect of Halliday's category-and-scale grammar. In a nutsell, the background is the following. Simplifying somewhat, Hallidayan grammar in the mid-1960s had two basic clause types: alpha clauses for main clauses and beta clauses for subordinate ones. But I argued, consider the following two sentences:

1. Jane has to go and see the doctor.
2. Jane has to go to see the doctor.

According to the model, the first would be analysed alpha-alpha and the second alpha-beta, even though the sentences looked much more similar than that. However, when I raised this problem in a written paper, the tutor dismissed my criticism as a trivial anomaly, suggesting that it would be more appropriate for a diploma student to follow the party-line. Hallidayans are rather often like that in my experience.

Another strong course was that in articulatory phonetics taught by a middle-aged lady called Miss Honikmann. She was firm, clear, precise and demanding, requiring us regularly to go to the phonetics department to assign International Phonetic Alphabet (IPA) symbols to sounds we were given on a bunch of old 78-speed records. Particularly demanding was the voiceless fricative record because it was worn out and contained lots of hissing background white noise. So, we struggled to identify against this hiss, various "sss", "shshsh", "khkh" and "aukh" sounds. I spent hours down in the basement listening to these in the cubicle, and in the end got them nearly all right, much to Miss

Honikmann's surprise and approval. I didn't do so well on the phonetics final examination, which largely consisted of a read aloud passage (each phrase two or three times) to be transcribed into IPA. Towards the end, the Head of Phonetics, who was giving the exam, suddenly developed a speech impediment and what was "footsteps" became "foothshlepthsh" and, for the life of me, I couldn't remember when I needed it the phonetic symbol for that Welsh palatal voiceless fricative that you hear in all those Welsh place names that begin with double "L".

One of my new friends taking the diploma had opted for a short elective on dialectology, the highlight of which was a visit to an isolated farmhouse high in the Yorkshire dales. After a typical high tea, the small group visited the barn where the instructor asked the elderly farmer to give him the names of certain pieces of equipment. He pointed to a harrow and the farmer said "harrow", and he pointed a plough and the farmer said "plough". Then my friend overheard the instructor whispering to the farmer, "I'm going to ask you again, but this time tell us your father's name for it". So, he pointed to another harrow and the farmer said, "Arr, tha' be a glebe-rake" and when a plough was pointed to, he replied "Arr, tha' be an ol' clodbungler". As my friend observed, a career as a dialectologist didn't seem to have much of a future.

33

Napoleon's Marshals

Two of my closest friends on the course were Phillip Janetta and his wife Libby. Phillip was one of the British Council Officers, whom I caught up with two years later in Ankara on my honeymoon, and whom I used to see on occasion years later when he had retired from the Council to run a small private school in south-east England. Phillip was a history buff and after a dinner at his rented house, Phillip would ask, as a parlour game, his guests to write down how many seventeenth-century battles they could remember, or nineteenth-century British prime ministers, or how many of Napoleon's Marshals we knew. It goes without saying, we guests always lost by a big margin. Anyway, before a final celebratory dinner after the exams, one of the regular group said, "Why don't we bone up on Napoleon's Marshals and tempt Phillip to play the Marshal's game and beat him at it?" So, we agreed and did our homework; on the earlier instance, I had got just three (Ney, Soult and Marmont). So, after dinner that evening, one of my colleagues mildly and mischievously declared, "Hey, Phillip, after all your linguistics, I bet you have forgotten most of Napoleon's Marshals that you once knew. Shall we have a reprise?" Phillip rose to the bait, immediately assented, and we all started scribbling names down on a piece of paper. I think all three of us guests got at least 20 of Napoleon's 26 Marshals, while Phillip managed about 18. Much merriment ensued when we revealed our plot.

Years later I came across a vaguely comparable anecdote about Maurice Bowra, the longtime Warden of Wadham College, Oxford from 1938 to 1970. Sir Maurice was a well-known polymath and every evening at high table the young dons were becoming increasingly frustrated at the way the head of the college tended to dominate the conversation whatever the subject. So they secretly decided to bone up on a topic that they thought might be even beyond the impressive knowledge of their Warden. They chose fourteenth-century Persian pottery and studied it up before subtly introducing it weeks later at high table. For example, a manipulated conversation ensued about the appropriateness of the attribution of a fourteenth-century Persian pottery plate coming up for auction at Sotheby's to the small Persian pottery at Rayy. Animated discussion followed, at which the Warden was uncustomarily silent. "We've got him", the younger members of college whispered to each other. However, when a silence at the dinner table eventually emerged, the Warden looked down from his position at the head of table to his fellows and observed, "I am glad to see that you young gentlemen have been profiting from my anonymous article in the *Encyclopedia Brittanica* on mediaeval Persian pottery".

34

Agostino

Diploma A students were required to write a thesis, and I chose to study small "absolute clauses" in Italian, and the ways they were translated into English. In doing so, I was much influenced by Ian Catford's remarkable little volume entitled *A Linguistic Theory of Translation*, which had just been published. (Ian I got to know quite well when I joined the department of Linguistics at Michigan in the mid-1980s.) I analysed Moravia's novella *Agostino*, and its Penguin translation. Unfortunately, I have long lost my own copy of the thesis, and in the end I decided not to bother Leeds University to see if they had retained their copy in the back of some dusty cupboard. I can't in fact remember too much about the text, although I do know I managed to insert, for the first time in my life, the adjective *eponymous* into the opening chapter. The basic content of the thesis is clearer; the "absolute" clauses I was searching for were like the following:

> Andato in cucina, aprí il frigo
> (Gone into the kitchen, he opened the fridge)

Although such clauses are possible in several European languages, they are not really acceptable in English; as a result, in English they tend to be re-expressed in various ways:

> He went into the kitchen and opened the fridge
> Having gone into the kitchen, he opened the fridge
> When/after he went into the kitchen, he opened the fridge

I am guessing I found close to a hundred of such clauses in Moravia's text and, using various techniques, traced down their translation equivalents, and was able, I believe, to establish that certain kinds of Italian context predisposed certain kinds of English translation. In this process, I was greatly helped by my supervisor, Tony Cowie, who became a well-known lexicographer. He took, I think, considerable pains to treat me as an equal in this enterprise, and one sign of this was his willingness to admit that certain of his suggestions didn't pan out in practice. There were valuable lessons here for the later years when I found myself in supervisor or advisor roles. I believe Tony gave the thesis a pretty good mark and it certainly served as a useful academic-apprentice exercise. Overall, I was led to believe that I performed adequately on the diploma, being placed towards the bottom of the top six. Little sign yet, then, of a moderately successful career in academia.

In the last four episodes, I have made occasional critical remarks about a few aspects of my post-graduate year at Leeds. On the whole, however, it turned out to be both an enjoyable and a valuable experience. I became seriously interested in language issues, particularly as they interfaced with language teaching issues, one sign of this being that I joined the Linguistics Society of America in order to get their journal *Language*. Indeed, the quarterly issues of this journal kept me vaguely *au courant* with linguistic developments over the next dozen years or so. Towards the end of my year in northern England, I found myself re-appointed to the University of Libya, but this time to the Engineering Faculty in the capital city, Tripoli, and this time as a lecturer rather than an assistant lecturer. Writing now in 2009, I am not quite sure how this came about, but I think that Professor Mitchell had something to do with it since I also received a small research grant of £200 a year under something he had orchestrated and which was called the "Libya-Leeds Link Scheme".

35

Unexpected new responsibilities

On a very hot September afternoon in 1966, I drove (in a Morris 1100 this time) up to the border post on the Libyan-Tunisian border. The border was miles from anywhere and the semi-desert stretched in all directions. The Libyan customs post consisted of a barrier across the road and small hut by its side. No other cars were in the vicinity and nobody seemed to be around. I stopped at the barrier and walked round to the shady side of the hut where a young customs officer was dozing in the afternoon heat. To my horror, I saw that the guardian of my entry to Libya had fifteen months earlier been a student who had been dismissed from the university, partly because I had refused to raise his failing mark in the English exam. "Ye Gods", I said to myself as I looked around at his uncomfortable, isolated and desolate surroundings, "this guy must surely hate me and will give me a sack of trouble". But instead, he jumped up, shook my hand warmly and said, "Welcome back to Libya, Mister John, you have time for a cup of tea?" To this day, I have never quite managed to work out this episode.

After a couple of weeks, I was settled in Tripoli and had started to prepare for classes for the first- and second-year Engineering students at the university. Suddenly, the Englishman who had been Head of the English Section at the college since its establishment was abruptly dismissed—and for reasons that I never fully understood. The Acting Dean had me in and said, "I am going to make you Head of Section because you are the only one with recent professional training". I was somewhat taken aback by this sudden promotion but, after some hesitation, I agreed to take on the new responsibilities. For one thing, early impressions of my colleagues were highly favorable. There were three other expatriate lecturers, a British language laboratory technician, and the locally hired American wife of the Libyan Dean of Science. The three lecturers were Patrick Lewis, a considerable Arabist, James Cormick, who had some useful background in Science, and Hugh Mildmay, who had some equally useful TEFL training. Secondly, there seemed quite a bit to do on the curriculum side. There was a 24-booth language laboratory but little suitable material for it. The previous head had purchased copies of Herbert's (1965) *The Structure of Technical English*, but we soon found that the exercise typology was severely limited (or "depauperate" as my botanist friends would say). Third, with my recent training in linguistics and ELT, I was raring to go on some creative materials development projects. For such tasks, I had brought with me a photocopy of Charles Barber's pioneering chapter entitled "Some measurable characteristics of modern scientific prose", as well as sundry professional books, including a copy of Noam Chomsky's brilliant *Aspects of a theory of syntax*. Fourthly, the only way I then knew how to lead was by example; if I started to do the basic linguistic research and/or started to develop our own materials, others would hopefully follow. (Indeed, this lead-by-example style has remained with me ever since; the only thing I later added was some penchant for "management by wandering around"). However, with these new and unexpected commitments, I am afraid that the Leeds-Libya Link research project sadly languished.

The College of Engineering was essentially English-medium. The textbooks were in English, as were the student exams and assignments; lectures were in English, or in a mixture of English or Arabic if given by the many Egyptian faculty; social and administrative conversations were typically in Arabic. There were the usual degree-granting engineering departments, and three service sections, English, mathematics, and workshop technology. We were given five hours of English for the first-year students and three hours for the second year. As I wrote in a retrospective on my Tripoli experience, published in 1976:

> The students had studied English at school for about six hours a week for six years and had, on university entry, the expected EFL post-secondary strengths and weaknesses—reasonable vocabulary, grammatical "knowledge" and graphology, the basis of a serviceable written and aural comprehension, serious interference problems, both linguistic and cultural, in their free written work, and quite understandable inhibitions about speaking English. ·

Given this situation, it could be concluded that, in terms of *student English need*, the traditional language skills could be ranked in decreasing order of importance as reading, listening, writing and speaking. However, I argued that, in terms of *English teacher classroom intervention*, the order should be writing, speaking, listening and reading. The students would get heavy exposure throughout their five-year degree to the last two skills. On the other hand, the two productive skills would probably not develop much without the direct intervention of the English section. In addition, a writing/speaking orientation would allow us to keep rather more within our scientific depth. And finally, the engineering faculty complained about the poor quality of written English in the students' final exams.

We set to work. James Cormick and I counted, following Barber's example, verb tenses in the textbooks, and also assembled vocabulary lists. One major investigation, I remember, was devoted to finding the 200 most common verbs in the first-year textbooks, where, inter alia, we were surprised to discover that there weren't 200 different verbs in the mathematics volume! We noticed that in exams, students were typically asked to undertake tasks such as Describe the A.C. Dynamo, or Define the stress, strain and elastic limits. They also had to make statements about dimensions and properties, to make comparisons, and use the passive in accounts of procedure. As a result, we included materials on all these topics. Later, we included work on commentaries on tables and graphs. Over the next two years, the first- and second-year writing courses began to take shape. Sometime early in 1967, Richard Yorkey of the American University in Beirut asked me to write a piece for his small *TEFL* journal. I adapted the materials I had been working on for teaching the uses of *for forty years* and *since 1937* and *in 1937* and *forty years ago*—the *for/since* being particularly difficult for many non-native speakers of English. This was my first ESL publication.

36

An attempted dismissal

Meanwhile, there were the reel-to-reel language lab materials to think about. After about a year experimenting with various exercise types and with various kinds of material, we began to wonder what other labs were up to in other universities in the Middle East, so the lab technician (Hillary Webb) and I designed a questionnaire to send out to the 50 or so labs we thought to be in existence in the region. I went to the Assistant Dean and asked if the college would cover the costs of mailing out our several-page questionnaire. He refused, saying, "Mr Swales, you are here to teach not to do research". I attempted to argue that our project would ultimately be related to pedagogy and might indeed improve our teaching, but he would have none of it. I continued to argue, but he curtly told me that the issue was closed and asked me to leave. I paid the postage costs myself and our relationship remained frosty for months afterwards. At the end of the 1967–1968 year, my two-year contract was up and at the crucial Deans' meeting, the Assistant Dean attempted to have me dismissed for "insubordination"; however, his superior apparently argued that I was to be congratulated for the English Section's "tailor-made courses"—the first time I had heard this useful phrase—and the Dean of Science apparently said that if Engineering didn't want me, the Faculty of Science would be happy to offer me a contract. My contract was extended two years.

The incident recounted above is 40 years old and took place in a distant land, but the phenomenon of administrative attempts to drive a disjunction between research-type investigations and classroom teaching in English for Academic Purposes contexts has reverberated throughout my academic life. For example, in early 2008, I re-encountered it in Hong Kong, when I was asked to evaluate the work of the Department of English; indeed, at the very time of writing, a review committee at Michigan is pondering what activities beyond straightforward teaching and advising EAP lecturers may legitimately undertake. Administrators seem to have difficulty recognizing that specialized language teaching materials require a lot of groundwork (not to speak of creativity), nor do they seem to appreciate that simply teaching the same old material year after year almost inevitably leads to boredom and burn-out.

37

Attempting to learn Arabic

This was mostly a sore trial, partly because, as in much of the developing world, the people whom one wanted to talk to generally spoke English or some other European language better than I was ever likely to speak Arabic. In effect, this was the sociolinguistic negative of living in a major urban centre. (The people who learned serviceable Libyan Arabic while in the country were those, like the Peace Corps, who lived and worked in rural areas.) Nevertheless, I fitfully persevered, but struggled especially with the vocabulary. However, one winning strategy I developed was to buy the object whose name I was attempting to learn. I still remember going to a stationery shop in order to buy a *kharaama* or hole-punch. (There was, by the way, one such shop in the centre of Benghazi that in English called itself, with this spelling "Everybody's Stationary"—according to local wags an apt enough summation of life in Cyrenaica at that time.) My practice was to rehearse beforehand my expected conversation with the shop keeper, and to make sure that when I got there I repeated the target lexical item enough times to remember it. To this day: *kharaama* = hole punch.

The best Arabic teacher I ever had was Tony Dudley-Evans, a lecturer in English in the Faculty of Science and who had an undergraduate degree in Arabic from the famous School of Oriental and African Studies at London University. The day before our lessons (James Cormick also was learning Arabic), Tony would drop off copies of the local newspaper at our flats with a passage selected for homework. Under Tony's guidance, we made some headway toward reading the local newspaper, which was written in Modern Standard Arabic; however, the only items that I could read with any ease were what I always thought of as "non-news items". There were lots of these and they typically went—in translation—like this:

Yesterday, the Under-secretary for Trade and Commerce, Dr Othman Ho-dali, had a meeting at the Ministry of Finance with his brotherly counter-part from Tunisia, Essaied Ahmed Maghrabi. In the three hour meeting, they discussed several matters of mutual interest in a constructive and cor-dial manner. (The Libyan News Agency.)

Tony will appear and re-appear in later chapters as we became close friends and colleagues. I never saw James after Tripoli, but I heard of him from time to time. The last I heard he was teaching English at Bir Zeit University in the West Bank.

38

Van Milne visits and the Libyan revolution

Some time late in 1968, we received a visit from van Milne, the com-missioning ESP/ELT editor for Thomas Nelson, who was touring the Middle East, partly to sell textbooks, and partly to seek out potential manuscripts. I showed him the writing course materials I had been pri-marily responsible for, and he expressed considerable approval, adding that if I ever shaped them into a coherent textbook, he would consider publishing it. At the time of his visit, I didn't pay too much attention, as we were busy with other things, including trying to keep the language lab running. (Hillary and I could sometimes be found on weekends, trying to replace diodes with a soldering iron.)

Early in the morning of September 1, 1969, my wife woke me to say that she could hear shooting down the street, but I turned over mutter-ing, "It's only the navy patrol boats doing their usual shooting practice off-shore". (We lived near the beach.) She went up on the roof and saw some soldiers running into the radio station down the road, which was off the air. This was the beginning of the largely bloodless Libyan revo-lution, and the streets for days were full of cheering crowds. The uni-versity was closed for three months, an 8 PM curfew was imposed

(James Cormick was caught a couple of times and had to spend the night in a police station), and alcohol banned. In effect, university and social life was severely curtailed, and I said firmly to myself, thinking of van Milne's offer, "Well, it's either now or never". I got down to the demanding and laborious work of editing a mass of teaching material into a suitable textbook form. I was done by early 1970, and I sent the manuscript to van Milne, who agreed to publish it "as is". It appeared in 1971 as *Writing Scientific English* (WSE), with the sub-title of *A text-book of English as a Foreign Language for students of Physical and Engineering Sciences*. It did well for many years (my 1982 copy is from the eighth printing) and sold well over 50,000 copies. It went out of print in the mid-1980s when Thomas Nelson was taken over by another firm, and some incoming accountant-type arbitrarily killed off all books that weren't selling X thousand a year. There was also a pirated Chinese version, rumoured to consist of 600,000 copies, and an official Japanese version, which is still in print. (Indeed, just the other day I received a royalty cheque for 123 pounds.) I have copies of both. As I was writing this, out of curiosity, I checked whether there were any used copies available on Amazon. There was just one, carrying the not unprincely price tag of $65.95! Maybe it has, unbeknownst to me, become a collectible item, although I rather suspect it is simple price escalation based on rarity.

Interestingly, the book was successful largely because it was transitional. Let me try and explain this apparent paradox. WSE had a strong grammatical base, largely based on our studies of the prevailing grammatical structures in textbooks. Apart from one or two personal indulgences, it covered the ground the students needed to know in ways that fairly traditional ESL instructors were familiar with. On the other hand, it also had certain functional elements (e.g. definitions and descriptions of how things work) and, toward the end, began to explore aspects of textual cohesion. In effect, it was new but not too new. Other factors that may have appealed to more serious instructors were the fact that the 12 units did not have a uniform structure but were shaped as seemed most appropriately toward the topic they dealt with, as well as the fact that the exercises were varied and at times not without cognitive challenge. One feature that I liked, but I don't think anybody else ever paid much attention to, was a penchant for motivated exclusions. To illustrate, here is a short extract from the preface:

> The reader will not find, for example, any detailed discussion of Conditional Clauses. This is because the preliminary analysis suggested that the hypothetical and counter-factual types of condition are not, in fact, either typical or useful at the level of straightforward description. The 'simple' conditional Clause is needed, but the factors affecting the choice of Present Simple or 'will' are highly complex and not fully understood at the present time.

I don't know whether these two claims would stand up to further validation, or indeed whether they might still apply to later science and engineering textbooks, but they do provide an early indication of my interest—not so usual for a linguist—in what is *not* chosen, *not* written and *not* said. Later, this whole issue of discoursal silence would loom large in my thinking.

When the university eventually re-opened, Moammar El-Ghaddafi made a visit in which he urged the science and engineering colleges to convert to Arabic medium as part of the new Libyan nationalism. The largely Egyptian teaching faculty were all in favour, since it would give them a near-monopoly on these comparatively well-paid positions. However, the Libyan students were solidly against, and the Arabicization policy was shelved for the time being. A few days after the leader of the revolution's visit, I asked one of the student leaders about the students' rejection of Ghaddafi's proposal. He looked at me with a wry smile and replied, "Well, mister John, if you were single and 23 like me, would you rather do your master's degree in Cairo or in California?"

39

Language laboratory materials and service courses: Problems of tape course design for science students

This was the title of a shortish article I wrote in my last months in Tripoli and which was published the following year in the *Audio-visual Language Journal*. As I look back, I am struck by the fact that the second part of the title mentions "problems", but has nothing to say about "solutions". I would consider this unusual in the applied linguistics field where it is customary in our presentations and publications to, as it were, put our best foot forward; in other words, we tend to highlight what worked and to conveniently fail to mention what didn't. (There are, of course, a few exceptions to this generalization in ESP, Colin Barron being a notable example.)

That said, much of the article is, in fact, taken up with reporting what *did* work; here is an extract:

> There are clear motivational advantages in presenting some of the necessary practice with the empty auxiliary "do" in this way:
>
> > This is a typical day in the life of Dr Jones, but the times given are always two hours early. Reply as shown.
> > He gets up at 6 o'clock .... I don't think he does; he doesn't get up till 8.
> > He has breakfast at 7 o'clock. ....
> > He gets to college at 8 o'clock ....
> > (Etc.)
>
> The small piece of problem-solving (adding on two hours) gives such an exercise an attraction for our students that is lacking in a straightforward make-negative structural presentation. There is some evidence that this drill, which is flanked by less contextualized material, is remembered better both in terms of human activity and in terms of retention of grammatical structure; and, after all, retention of material is the first step towards that

Transfer of Training by which the Language Laboratory must ultimately be judged, and is at present being judged unfavourably.

Pretty fair comment, I reckon, for something written in 1970.

The other extract I have selected gets closer to the substance of the title:

> In a questionnaire-survey of language laboratories [in the Middle East] carried out by H. H.Webb and myself, we found that at least 70 labs have so far been bought, of which around 50 were primarily intended for the teaching of English. I write "were" advisedly, because 20 or so are apparently no longer working. Half of the remainder are viewed by those who run them as a dire affliction—an attitude that is likely to rub off on the students who use them. The relatively few that function well, in nearly every case do so because the staff in charge have found the time and interest to produce their own material. These L-Ls are usually in universities and training colleges where the teaching loads are less and the holidays longer; organizations that rely on taped material from outside the area, such as the British Council, U.S.I.S and many private language schools, make a poorer showing. The message to the purchasing authorities is clear: don't buy a lab until you know where to buy effective material for it; if there isn't any, don't buy a lab until you can buy the staff who can give you that material.

There is a certain punchy directness about the above extract, although the "dire affliction" comment now seems a bit overdone.

I have included these two longish extracts from this early publication for a couple of reasons. They show, I would like to believe, a reasonably articulate and maturing writing style focused on what seems to be emerging as my chosen professional specialty and identity. More importantly, they indicate certain traits in my thinking that had become consolidated at the Tripoli campus of the University of Libya and would largely remain thereafter. These would include a belief in "tailor-made materials"; a belief in the need for appropriate language and linguistic research to underpin those materials; an interest in challenging tasks; and a hope that research and teaching would be synergistic.

40

Envoi to Libya

I would not like to conclude this chapter without briefly mentioning some more general incidents that I remember from my Tripoli days. The first occurred soon after my arrival when I accompanied Patrick Lewis on a carpet-buying expedition to the *souk*. We entered a shop and bargaining commenced, with Patrick, in fluent Libyan Arabic, berating the products on offer with comments like "Wallahi, you cannot expect me to pay that price for this unhappy piece of badly-woven sheep dung". The back-and-forth continued for about 20 minutes, with a growing crowd of onlookers listening to the dialogue between Patrick and the merchant. When eventually agreement was reached, the crowd broke into spontaneous applause at the rhetorical performance of the *farangi*.

A second took place when I was attending at the local cinema a showing of the film of Thomas Hardy's *Far from the Madding Crowd*. As readers may remember, the film opens with a scene of a flock of sheep being driven off a cliff to their deaths by a marauding dog. This scene caused a huge audience reaction in Tripoli, with moans, yells and cries at the disaster from the almost entirely male audience. I was very forcefully reminded by this outburst of emotion and by the strong empathy for the unfortunate shepherd that Libya, despite its new oil and its growing cities, still remained at that time a country with deep and strong pastoral roots and traditions.

Colloquial Arabic has a common expression *fursa sai?ida*, which literally translates as "happy chance", and is commonly used on meeting people, especially unexpectedly or for the first time. So, students might pass me on their bicycles and shout "habby shance, mister John". It happened I knew a Libyan secondary school teacher who had a remarkably elaborate vocabulary in English, but with little appreciation of the pragmatics of that language. Anyway, one day in 1967, my wife mentioned that she thought she might be pregnant for the first time, but would I please not say anything to anybody until she was sure. A day or so later, we were walking in downtown Tripoli, when my Libyan acquaintance came up to us, shook our hands, and said "auspicious occasion", at which my wife muttered angrily, "I told you not to tell anybody!" I don't know whether I ever really persuaded her that I hadn't spilled the beans; rather, my friend, true to type, had just produced a pretentious translation of the Arabic expression *fursa sai?ida*.

In the summer of 1970, the final exit visa process became even more fraught than usual, because the large American base outside Tripoli was closing down. The Libyan authorities became worried (quite appropriately) that many domestic pets might be left behind, abandoned on the base or in the nearby residential areas. So yet another bureaucratic form was introduced for the visa, requiring expatriates leaving the country for good to show that they had made appropriate arrangements for their pets. This consisted of a section for your personal details, a photo of the animal, and the signature of a vet for euthanasia, or of the new owner who had offered to take it on. This process was not too arduous if you *had* a pet, but presented serious problems if you didn't own one! Since quite a number of us were leaving the College of Engineering that summer, we established a system of the "final exit cat", which was copied many times and passed from one individual to another, along with the requisite signature, as our various departure dates became imminent.

FOUR

A Mistake in Leeds and a Recovery in Khartoum

41

The Overseas Educational Studies Group (OESG)

Before we left Tripoli, I had obtained a lectureship in the Institute of Education at the University of Leeds. I suspect I got the job for a variety of reasons, one being that I had the *WSE* textbook in press. I was actually appointed to the OESG (The Overseas Educational Studies Group), which offered three diplomas for overseas educators, one of which was Teaching English Overseas (TEO) and where a large minority of the participants were Sudanese secondary school teachers. Clearly, in this circumstance, my experience with ESL in the Arab World would likely have been considered a plus. Third, I would be replacing Pablo Foster, who was on his way to Tunisia to work on a new English textbook for Tunisian secondary schools, and I suspect that Pablo put in a good word for me.

So in the autumn of 1970, closing in on my 32nd birthday, I had obtained a permanent lecturership in a large and well-known British university. I was, so it seemed, set for life. In those days, the position of lecturer was "the career grade", by which was meant that this was the rank most people could expect to have for all their academic life. Only about 10 percent of the university posts were for professors (who often were also heads of departments), while another 25 percent or so were allocated to senior lecturers or readers, the remaining two-thirds would be lecturers and would remain so. The OESG in the early 1970s was staffed by about seven lecturers and one senior lecturer, most of these colleagues being considerably older and nearly all with experience as educators of various kinds during the closing years of the British colonial administrations around the world. The other "Young Turk"—and he was more of a young Turk than I aspired to be—was Steve Whiteley, who had recently been teaching at the University of Dar Es Salaam in Tanzania. Anyway, soon after our arrival, we attempted to democratize the unit by suggesting that the "Staff Toilet" be made available to all in the building, arguing in effect that the students taking one of our diploma courses were all "staff" back in their home countries. No dice. We were firmly rebuffed by what we considered to be "the old guard" only too anxious, we muttered, to protect their sanitary privileges.

42

Teaching on the TEO etc

One of my main teaching assignments was the course in ESL teaching methods at the secondary school level, where I made much use of a recently published book by Bright and McGregor entitled *Teaching English as a Second Language* and subtitled *Theory and techniques for the secondary stage*. Bright had worked in the Sudan and Uganda, while McGregor had spent most of his professional life in the latter country. I was sometimes rather uncomfortable with this assignment, often being uncertain about the applicability of the teaching techniques I was advocating in secondary school systems as diverse as Sudan, Nepal, Hong Kong and Malaysia. On the other hand, I was particularly impressed by what the authors had to say about ESL reading, not something I had been much involved with until now. Here is an extract from the section on reading lesson techniques (and remember they were talking about large classes in African secondary schools):

> The passage should first be read silently by the pupils. It is direct response to the black marks on paper that we want to improve. We do not want to train pupils to read things aloud before they can understand them. It is necessary to deny them the help of the teacher's voice. The slowest readers should not be given time to complete the passage. If we wait for them, most pupils will feel no pressure at all to read quickly. The slow readers will perhaps read a little faster themselves next time and will not suffer unduly in any case because there is time during the questioning for them to look at the text again.

This advocacy of the largely silent reading class struck me forcefully, although I didn't have any real opportunity to put anything into practice until a couple of years later.

I also offered two short elective courses, one on Modern Syntactic Theories (if you can believe that), the other for math teaching diploma students on The Language of Mathematics, partly based on the analyses James Cormick and I had undertaken back in Tripoli. More interesting for me was a course that Steve Whiteley and I developed in our second year at Leeds entitled Professional Communications, which dealt with differences between spoken and written English, and with the linguistic characteristics of certain genres (although we certainly didn't use that term) that we felt might be useful for educators. One particularly successful activity was practice in taking the minutes of meetings, which involved participants listening to simulated meetings in the university's excellent language lab setup. Designing these activities involved me in those pedagogically oriented text-task sequences that would become an increasingly important part of my professional life.

Similarly engaging was a collaboration with an Egyptian professor on secondment from the American University in Cairo, Dr Salah El-Arabi, with whom I developed some "bicultural tapes" on differences between expectations among British and Arab populations. We constructed dialogic scenarios such as receiving a gift, with a *sotto voce* voice-over containing such mutterings as, "Why doesn't she open it and see what it is?!" Here we were assisted by Brian Page, the outstanding director of the language lab. Looking back, we could easily have published an article based on this work.

My other major activity was teaching a shortish course on "materials development" (where I could make use of my Libyan experience in developing writing and speaking activities), which was seen as a preparation for supervising in the spring and early summer a fair number of the TEO Diploma students' Long Essays, a kind of mini-thesis running to some 30–40 pages on some topic hopefully of interest to the student. On the whole, this activity was a challenge for both supervisee and supervisor. Few of the students had ever attempted anything as ambitious as this and, despite considerable staff efforts to get respectable outcomes, most of the final products were of rather indifferent quality. I generally supervised those diplomands who wanted to undertake an inquiry that involved language (or specialized language) in some way, such as an analysis of how dimensions are expressed in English and how these expressions might be taught to non-native speakers of the language. On occasion of course I did have students who produced really interesting long essays; I remember one from Nepal and one from Fiji, both of whom we consequently recommended for master's courses, but in general this was tough sledding.

The other major aspect of my job was to accompany the students on school visits, so they could observe the wonders of the English educational system in action. Among other things, this involved polite and stilted conversations with head teachers about the way their schools solved its problems. The organizer of this activity tried hard to include some visits to rural schools since many of our students would be returning to rural areas, and at least one visit to a school in a deprived inner city area of Leeds. At this last, I remember sitting, with my TEO observers, at the back of some science class where the teacher was a real martinet. At one moment, a youth spoke out of turn and the instructor barked at him, "Murgatroyd, when I want your opinion, I will rattle the bars of your cage".

43

Two talks

Sometime in my second year, I was asked to give a talk to the staff of the Institute and I chose to speak on the language of science—essentially an expansion of Barber's 1962 chapter entitled "Some measurable characteristics of modern scientific prose". I was pretty nervous, I recollect, and opened with some comments that the talk would only consist of some preliminary thoughts and findings and sundry other apologies. In the question period, a lecturer called Douglas Barnes, whom I didn't really know at that time, asked some probing questions about science textbooks and the speech used in science teaching, querying in particular whether children discussing science needed to use the formal vocabulary found in textbooks. After the seminar closed with some doubtless polite applause, an older lecturer, a gruff Yorkshireman I think called Bradshaw, came up to me and said:

> Swales [a not atypical term of address at that time], let me give you a piece of advice. Never apologise when beginning a talk. It will never do you any good, and will only do you harm. All it ever does is lower the audience's expectations of what they are about to hear.

Memorable counsel that I have followed religiously ever since, and which I have passed on to quite a few of my own students and junior colleagues, and to others that I have met at conferences and in various departments around the world.

The other talk I best remember from my days at Leeds was given by Douglas Barnes, whom I have already mentioned. Douglas had written a profound and penetrating little book called *Language, the Learner, and the School*, in which he had, among other things, contrasted the *transmission* of scientific knowledge in taught lessons with the *interpretation* of scientific data in peer-group schoolchild discussions. During this talk, Douglas played some tape-recordings of small groups of pre-teens talking together about science concepts. After his extract, he made no comment, often allowing long and uncomfortable silences to develop, to the extent that we all wondered what the hell was going on. Right at the end, he explained that he didn't want to make any interpretive comments himself because he had found in the science classes he studied that the teacher quickly coming in with the "right" answer had all too often stifled intellectual curiosity among the class. Although, as a teacher, I am basically too impetuous to fully adopt Douglas' policy, it certainly taught me something about the importance of "wait time". Recently, I looked Douglas Barnes up on the web and found he had retired from Leeds as a Reader in 1989. More importantly though, his work strongly survives; a recent Google Scholar search shows 245 hits for a later edition of *Language, Learner, and the School* and 646 hits for a later book entitled *From Communication to Curriculum.* He was a modest and very thoughtful man, as well as being something of a pioneer in discourse analysis. However, my attempts to interest people at Michigan's School of Education in the publications of Douglas Barnes have so far proved largely futile.

44

Cairo, Copenhagen, Cairo, Alexandria, Khartoum, Bakht-Ar-Ruda

In the summer of 1972 I was invited by the Ford Foundation to spend six weeks at the American University of Cairo (AUC) working with the service English staff on developing EAP materials. I linked up with Saleh El-Arabi where we gave, if memory serves, a joint workshop at AUC based on our bicultural tapes that we had developed a year or so earlier. Most of my time, however, was spent with a group of about four lecturers revising the English for Science courses. As best as I remember, the existing materials were largely based on American textbooks for teaching technical communication, and we devoted long hours to adapting these materials so that they would be more suitable for an Arab and Arabic-speaking student body. Definitions and relative clauses were, I recollect, two areas where we produced extensive supplementary materials.

In the late summer of that year, I went (accompanied by my wife) to the Applied Linguistics Congress in Copenhagen. I hadn't submitted an abstract; indeed, it never occurred to me to do so. I attended, as part of the milling crowd, quite a number of presentations, but didn't ask a single question or make a single comment. I did meet Larry Selinker, the leader of the "Washington University" school of ESP, but he, as an official presenter, had access to the university's staff cafeteria, whereas members of the *hoi polloi* like me had to pay highly inflated prices at specially arranged catering sites elsewhere on campus. I remember I did hear an excellent talk by David Wilkins, whom I had known in my early days in Libya. And observing the stylish way in which he presented probably inhibited me further. Finally, on one occasion, a crowd of about 30 of us had assembled to hear a particular speaker, who apparently didn't seem to be there. A middle-aged, smart-looking British gent offered to find out if the speaker had registered. He came back a few minutes later, saying "no". He then immediately offered to "ventriloquize" what the speaker might have said, given the abstract; he proceeded to talk elegantly in fully extempore manner for about fifteen minutes, explicating the topic. At the close, I asked the person sitting next to me who on earth this amazing paragon was, "Oh that's Professor Peter Strevens" came the reply, one of the major pioneers of British applied linguistics. So, my first major conference was a pretty dispiriting experience on a personal level. I didn't seem able to engage with the events in any meaningful way. Looking back, this was a time in my life when I would really have benefited from an academic mentor who could have pushed me along, or at least pushed me forward.

Over the 1972–73 Christmas vacation, the British Council asked me to run four-day in-service courses in English for Science for secondary school English teachers in Cairo and Alexandria, spending the remaining day of the week observing scientific English classes in Schools. I was also invited to spend a few days in the Sudan before returning. My visits to Cairene and Alexandrian secondary schools were, to select an ambiguous word, "interesting". The secondary school teachers, typically with a humanities background, had been recruited to teach the new scientific English syllabus as part of Egypt's effort to improve its Anglophone technological prowess, which was at that time thought to be both a necessary and a sufficient condition for economic development. ("Invest in human capital" was the mantra of that time.)

Alas, as I observed the scientific classes, these aspirations were subverted by the teachers who consistently turned the scientific processes soberly described in the textbooks into opportunities for "humanizing" and thereby subverting those processes. Student descriptions of oil extraction were embellished by crayon drawings of pretty oases in which they were situated. The standard processes were turned into narratives of tough and heroic engineers wresting oil from recalcitrant nature. Although I was sympathetic to the teachers' predicament of having to cope with a new syllabus devoted to a variety of English for which they were under-prepared, I concluded in my report that much more inservice training would be required to make the innovation a success.

In Khartoum, I made a couple of visits to the university for discussions with Don Porter and Bill Crewe, who were in charge of the Scientific English Section in the Faculty of Science. There they had produced a reading comprehension textbook based on material used in the first-year science courses and published by the University of Khartoum Press. The selection of texts was excellent, but they explained that the comprehension exercises had to be relatively simple and largely traditional since most of the actual instructors were untrained, being the wives of European expatriates and working on local contracts. Although I might have questioned this particular curricular decision, the "teachability" issue would continue to loom large in ESP/EAP materials development for years to come.

I also made a brief visit on a dusty Sudan Railways train to Shendi, a small town further up the Nile some four slow hours north of the capital. There I stayed with a couple of teachers who had taken the TEO Diploma my first year. With that wonderful enthusiasm for their profession that many Sudanese English teachers of their generation had, they dragged me to observe their classes, saying things like "Mister John, please come and see me teach Conditional 3". I also concocted a couple of sample lessons, but the school had at that time no photocopy paper. So one of the teachers and I went to the local stationery shop where I bought two reams, the whole stock in town. As we left, my colleague said, "Careful, John, you will single handedly cause inflation in Shendi by doing things like that!" On my second and final evening, we went to the Teachers' Club in Shendi for soft drinks and cakes. At the entrance, there was a sandpit with a large number of walking sticks and staffs lying on the ground. It was explained to me that the tradition was that these potential weapons had to be left outside in case political discussions inside became overheated.

In my final days in the Sudan, I went in a Ministry of Education Landrover, along with a couple of ministry officials, to the famous teacher training institute at Bakht-Ar-Ruda. This involved pretty well an all-day trip, going down bumpy tracks through the Gezira, taking a ferry across the White Nile to Ed Dueim, and then a short, equally bumpy, drive to the institute. The institute had been established in 1934, largely by V. L. Griffiths, who published a 1953 book about it entitled *An Experiment in Education*. Griffiths wanted the institute to be off the beaten track, away from the attractions and distractions of city life, and to better prepare the trainees for working in rural schools in an atmosphere devoted to educational matters. J. A. Bright, who had been the Chief Inspector there for many years, once summed up his Bakht-Ar-Ruda experience with these words: "The worst place in the world to live, but the best place in the world to work". Indeed, the products of the institute had a considerable *esprit de corps*, and they used to refer to themselves by the batch number of the in-service course they had attended. So you would hear, "You were Batch 26? Well, I'm Batch 29".

I stayed for my two nights there with two young British VSOs (Voluntary Service Overseas) in a staff house on the campus. I remember them showing me extracts from the manual for living in rural Sudan by the head office; one I remember went something like this, "Milk may be a problem; you may be able to buy tins of Carnation in the local shop; alternatively, you can keep a goat". On the last night, we all met up at the Staff Club for an evening meal, tea and general conversation. (Again, the sticks and staffs were left outside in a sandpit.) When we broke up at about ten in the evening, I strode off across the dark campus to the staff house where I was staying; when I looked back I noticed that all the Sudanese had their flashlights out and lit, were carrying their sticks and staffs, and were walking gingerly down the various paths. "Odd", I thought to myself, "they didn't seem that old". On the journey back I mentioned this behavior to the ministry officials. "Oh", they said. "Didn't you know? Bakht-Ar-Ruda is notorious for all the poisonous snakes that live there and emerge on the paths at night". "Now you tell me", I muttered.

45

A sense of ennui

I was now into my third year at the Leeds institute and beginning to experience a sense of academic and professional dissatisfaction. I would write nothing during my three years there, except for a small piece published at the end of 1973 in the British Council journal *ELT Documents*. This was based on my recent experiences in Cairo and Alexandria and was entitled "Introducing teachers to English for science and technology". While it was true that by now we had three small children and had bought and were trying to fix and furnish our first house, I didn't think these developments entirely explained my relative lack of initiative. Also, by my third year, accompanying diploma students on school visits was definitely becoming old, as were the joint struggles aimed at getting the diploma students to produce passable final Long Essays. Overall, I began to question my suitability for a long-standing career in teacher education. On the one hand, I missed the direct teaching of the English language, rather than talking about how best to do it all the time; on the other, my AUC summer experience had reminded me that I really relished the challenge of devising specialised language teaching materials and perhaps, indeed, had some small talent for this activity. Further impetus for change came from a visit from Ron Mackay, who at that time was involved in the EAP programme at Newcastle University, and with whom we had interesting discussions about this sub-field's development. In that last year, I was also invited to Edinburgh to meet with Patrick Allen and Henry Widdowson, who were about to embark on their "Focus" ESP series of textbooks for Oxford University Press. The first volume was in press and was to appear in 1974; based on my *WSE* credentials, I was asked whether I would like to contribute a volume to the series. I thought long and hard about this because there were certain features I really liked about the manuscript they showed me, but there were others that I thought, as an instructor, were more theoretically than pedagogically based. Since I was told that there would be little room for manoeuvre, I eventually declined. Nevertheless, I remained intrigued.

So, with these thoughts swirling in my mind, one day in spring 1973, I saw an advertisement for the joint position of Professor in English and Director of the English Language Servicing Unit at the University of Khartoum. ELSU was a newly established unit, partly funded by British Government aid money, designed to help a broader range of students survive in a largely English-medium university. I applied and was invited to an interview board at the British Council headquarters in London. On the board were Matt McMillan, previously a professor at the University of Khartoum and by now a leading light in the council's ELT division, and Mohammed Nur, the Educational Counsellor from the Sudan Embassy in London, as well as a number of other luminaries. Anyway, I must have done well since I was offered the position. Before going I had to pass a medical exam, and for this, one day I presented myself—for the first and last time—at a doctor's office in Harley Street (Harley Street being the address of the most prestigious and most expensive medical practitioners in London). An elderly gentleman poked and prodded in the usual way, explaining, as he did so, that he had been conducting these exams for British going out to the Sudan for years, going back to soon after the Second World War. It puzzled me then—and still does so now—that the Sudanese government, always so short of money, should have persisted with such an unnecessarily expensive medical check-up.

46

The English Language Servicing Unit (ELSU)

So I arrived in Khartoum with the surprising titles of "Professor" and "Director"—surprising in the sense that I had done little at least to merit the former. I also found out that I was one of the last two expatriate heads of unit, the other being a German in the School of Medicine, and that I was *ex officio* a member of the University Senate and of the Faculty of Arts Research Board. All this constituted a heady jump from my previous status as a plodding lecturer, and I quickly realized that I would have to extend myself in order to justify these elevations.

Don Porter and Bill Crewe had by then left, but ELSU still had—or would shortly have—a sizeable staff. Ian Pearson, who would later write the Focus Series textbook on Biology, had been appointed with me as Senior Applied Linguist, and other London appointments included Jim Croft, Phil Skeldon, and Arnold Spenser, later to be joined by Tony Bex and Paul Fanning. Local appointments included three women who ran the Economics Section: Angele Tadros, who would later write a fine PhD dissertation at Birmingham on "Predictive structures in economics texts", and two British women married to Sudanese, Gillian Hashim and Frances Daffa'allah. Other appointments included Andreas Lambrou, a Cypriot Sudanese, Jill Osman, and Arvid Kleppe, whose wife was a lecturer in Archeology. A number of Sudanese teaching assistants came and went, prominent among them, Anwar Wagialla and then El-Tayyeb El-Hassan, who would later to do a PhD in ESP at Aston University. We also soon acquired a secretary and a gofer/teaboy.

Office space was very tight; the Economics Section shared a small office, while the rest of us occupied one large office, which had originally been designed as a small classroom. In effect, this evolved into an open plan Japanese-style arrangement, with ten people or so at desks in the same room. This set-up thus provided a forum for the easy exchange of ideas and suggestions and fostered a good sense of group camaraderie.

In 1973, ELSU provided courses for first- and second-year students in the Faculties of Science and Economics. By 1978, when I left, we had expanded our offerings to include first- and second-year students in the faculties of Law (led by Arnold Spenser) and Architecture (Phil Skeldon and myself), first- and second-year students in the Medical Technicians' Institute in the Medical School (Paul Fanning and myself), and second-year students in the Department of History (Jim Croft), while Tony Bex was just starting to teach spoken academic English to the post-graduates in the recently created Graduate School.

47

Tales from the main office

One of my first jobs after arrival was running the meeting devoted to who would teach which of the 30 or so sections of Scientific English to the first-year science students. A good number of these consisted of two-hour classes scheduled from seven to nine in the morning. "Who could be persuaded to do those?" I wondered, and indeed new arrivals like me balked at such an early prospect. I needn't have worried because all of the 7.00–9.00 slots were quickly picked up by the old hands. By the time next year's schedule meeting had rolled around, I was one of the first to opt for these early classes. At this time of the day, the students had been up for more than an hour, had showered and said the first prayers of the Muslim day; all in all, they were very alive and attentive, and would become continuously less so as the day lengthened and became markedly hotter. Another advantage was that with a two-hour class behind you, often the teaching was done for the day and attention could turn to administration or R & D matters.

Arnold Spenser had, by 1975, devised an interesting collocational dictionary for the Law School entitled *Noun-Verb Expressions in Legal English* (with Arabic translations provided by a colleague); this explained, for example, that one *"submits* a plea", but *"files* a grievance". The book was due to be published in paperback by the University of Khartoum Press, but problems with supplies of paper and ink, problems with the compositor staff, and problems with the finances had greatly slowed the process—to Arnold's increasing frustration. Anyway, after we had finished our 7.00–9.00 classes, we usually asked our teaboy to go to the staff club and procure us sandwiches for breakfast (often gristly liver wrapped in whatever wrapping might be available). So, one day the teaboy returned with the sandwiches, whereupon we were both surprised and amused to discover that they had all been wrapped in discarded preliminary proofs of Arnold's book. Arnold was perhaps less than delighted, but we ragged him for days about what a great marketing ploy this was. "Imagine", we said, "all over the university, people will be intrigued by your proofs as they eat their sandwiches". And, in fact, Arnold was quite a salesman; after the book was published he managed to sell copies in bulk to both the Attorney General's Office and to the Police Academy.

Phil Skeldon was head of the Scientific English Section and was something of a master at the tricky logistics of keeping the section running. One strategy he developed was to try and obtain keys to as many of the Faculty's rooms as possible; instructors in other departments soon learnt that if—as quite often happened—they found themselves locked out of their classrooms, Phil might well have an immediate answer. So, in this way, connections were made, and favours made might one day be reciprocated in some way. He also was a canny hoarder of paper for duplicating, via laboriously typed stencils on a drum Gestetner. (We never got the photocopying machine the British Council gave us to work.) Paper was often in short supply, but Phil always managed to have enough for important occasions like the final year exams. In addition, he struggled to try and equip the office. One day, two filing cabinets (yes, filing cabinets!) arrived on a cart; he had discovered a workshop in the industrial area east of the Nile that had started making recycled cabinets out of expired car body panels. While they were not Steelcase®, they were a godsend as our activities became more complicated.

One day we were mostly in the office when there was a sudden commotion outside. A large number of bees had swarmed out of a hole in the trunk of one of the large trees on campus. (These, remember, were the so-called "killer" African bees.) Some employees ran off campus, others huddled in their cars with all windows tight shut, while others cowered in their offices. Not so the teaboy from the department next door. In next to no time, he was up the tree with a bucket and mug, had collected half a bucket-full of honey, and had descended before the bees started to return. Yet another indication of how local knowledge can surpass the accumulated expertise of the foreign educated; a reminder that knowledge in the university is oddly distributed, and that practical experience can be found in unexpected places.

48

A year of "bare" participles

Very soon after we arrived in Khartoum, I decided that, if I were to justify my lofty position, I had better crank up some kind of research agenda. Indeed, after three fallow years in Leeds, I was desperately anxious to do this. This strong wish to get started immediately probably influenced my choice of topic, or at least it seems so in retrospect. I started leafing through the chemistry textbook that all the first-year science students had to read and began to notice the occurrence of passive participles that were "bare"—that did not have any clause of phrase attached to them. Here are two italicized examples:

1) The curve *shown* is a heating curve corresponding to a uniform addition of heat.

2) The fact that the *emitted* light is intermittent hints that the electricity . . . .

As readers have doubtless noted, the first participle follows the noun while the second precedes it. As I subsequently wrote:

> The first aim of this paper is to try and ascertain the factors that affect the scientist's choice of pre- or post-modifying position for the 'bare' participle, and secondly—and much more diffidently—to look for factors that affect the scientist's decision to use such a participle, as against both its omission and as against a decision to include more information by using a participial phrase, prepositional or otherwise.

I should now confess that my main motivation was intellectual curiosity, rather than the pedagogical needs of ELSU's programme, even if I might have pretended otherwise at the time. After all, these participles were not likely to constitute a major comprehension problem for our students. There had, in fact, been a brief discussion of this topic in the large Quirk *Grammar*, which, I suspected, owed much to a 1967 article by the great American linguist, Dwight Bolinger. Bolinger had, *inter alia*, argued for a semantic difference between *the stolen jewels* and *the jewels stolen*, adding that we can say *deposited money*, but not *withdrawn money*, since withdrawal is not a culturally recognized permanent characteristic. However, as far as I knew, nobody had investigated this topic in scientific discourse.

So, with some assistance from Andreas Lambrou, I wrote out on file cards all the instances of "bare" participles that occurred in the first 350 pages of the textbook. It turned out that there were 257 of these, which I took home and spread out on table. (Shades of the coins from Euesperides!) Months passed as I struggled to make sense of the data, but eventually a picture began to emerge. Laboriously I wrote up my findings, typing them (with my Olympia portable) onto 24 foolscap stencils. The press produced a printed cover and a bit of binding, and about

50 copies (I think) were run off. The final title was "Notes on the function of attributive –*en* participles in scientific discourse".

The resulting working paper was divided into six sections, each headed by nothing more than those evasive roman numerals that I was fond of at that time. Here is the end of the opening section:

> In such inquiries [functional studies of scientific text] it sometimes appears that the Applied Linguist has produced evidence of usages of linguistic forms that have escaped the notice of grammarians, lexicographers and linguists. The elicitation of such 'new usages' is usually incidental and arises because the Applied Linguist sets himself a different task to the Linguist in response to a different sort of question. If, for example, he asks himself how he is to prepare material for a suitable English course for Arabic-speaking Dental Technicians, his investigation into the English language needs of such an occupational group may involve him in looking at language situations that have fallen outside traditional sources for the rules of English usage. The Theoretical Linguist's criticism that studies of this nature are trivial and superficial is, doubtless, completely justified in terms of the evolution of linguistic theory, but it is equally evident that the Applied Linguist's different frame of reference makes such a criticism irrelevant.

So there! I still like the forceful tone of this—as well as the fact that I have capitalized my chosen profession throughout. However, I am more rueful about the sexism inherent in the extract. Alas, at that time, I apparently believed, as John Bright had memorably observed a few years earlier, that "In English grammar, man embraces woman".

One of those "new usages" concerned the functions of the common scientific bare participle *given*. For example, my example (28) began "In a *given* experiment it is observed that . . . ". I then comment:

> In science, attribution is an important convention. The role of *given* in sentences like (28) and other similar ones is, therefore, to signal unmistakably that the convention is being suspended. It may or may not be the case that (28) describes actual experimental data, but whether there was actually

such an experiment or not is shown by *given* to be an inappropriate line of enquiry.

The trickier second aim of the paper was to see how these participles were functioning in continuous text. Even here I was able to make a little progress, as evidenced by this commentary following a quoted paragraph from the textbook:

Furthermore, the actual forms of language used in this extract would seem to suggest that the first reference to a visual display of some kind, especially where there may be several potential reference points, requires the use of a locative phrase (*in Figure 6.5; in Figure 6.6.*). It is also worth noting that in both instances the authors further cater for the reader's presumed need for textual reference by including initial locative phrases in the respective following sentences (*In this graph; In each of these experiments*). But a second reference (*The data shown*) no longer needs a precise reference to the text, and subsequently (*However, at low temperature*) reference to the data is presupposed.

As I concluded, "It would thus seem, on the evidence from the Chemistry text, that many of the grammarians' single-sentence citations are unusually heavily loaded with semantic differences that can be associated with pre- or post-nominal position". It would also seem that I was developing into a discourse analyst of specialized written texts.

I sent off copies to the small but growing number of people seriously interested in ESP around the world, such as Jack Ewer in Chile, Ron Mackay in Newcastle, and Henry Widdowson in Edinburgh. I also sent a copy to Dwight Bolinger at Stanford. Back came a typed air-mail letter from Palo Alto by return of mail (or what might pass for that in the Sudanese postal service). Bolinger made a number of highly sagacious comments, strongly indicating that he had reached an understanding of my data in a couple of hours, as opposed to the months I had taken. However, he also strongly encouraged me to continue this kind of work because he felt I had some talent for it. (This precious letter I believe still to be in my possession, but I have put it such a safe place that I have not been able to retrieve it!) Bolinger's careful reading and thoughtful response to a paper from an unknown person in the middle of eastern Africa was an act of considerable personal and professional generosity. (And remember I never had a so-called mentor.) I have never forgotten this expansive gesture, and in later life, I have tried to follow Bolinger's example by responding to requests for help, advice or information from young scholars or students from around the world, especially from those in similarly disadvantaged circumstances. And I have good reason to believe that many of those erstwhile junior scholars have been equally helpful to others as they have advanced in their profession.

49

Teaching developments

In the spirit of the Bright and McGregor passage quoted earlier, Ian Pearson and I tried to make the single-hour reading comprehension Scientific English class as quiet and self-paced as possible. We devised some pre-reading activities designed to prime their interest in the upcoming passage by asking them to predict what it might contain. We then focused on skimming and scanning exercises prior to the more intensive reading. We usually finished up with a vocabulary development section. More important, we tried to avoid a teacher-led lockstep situation in these classes, whereby everybody would be doing the same thing at the same time. We recognized that certain students would be faster and better readers than others. So, the classes were largely silent, with the students trooping up in a sporadic fashion to the teacher's desk in the front to check their responses after each major activity. In the spirit of Bright and McGregor, students who couldn't finish in the hour were asked to do so for homework.

The longer double-period was devoted to a range of activities, such as listening, grammar and writing. I developed the habit of trying to make sure that there were four or five activities spanning the two hours, believing that attention spans of more than 30 minutes were hard to achieve or maintain. At least one of these activities would require pair work, where the students could discuss the task in Arabic if they wished. One common activity was what we called "re-expression exercises", which went something like this:

Rephrase the content of this sentence, starting with the given expression:

Fresh water boils at a temperature of 100 degrees centigrade.

a) When...
b) The temperature at...
c) Fresh water has . . .

We (perhaps fondly) thought that we had invented this particular type of exercise; whether this was true or not, the students found it challenging and stimulating. It is I think quite widely recognized that learners with intermediate or upper-intermediate proficiency in a foreign language (like the first-year students at the U of K) can often find one way to express what they want to say or write, but have difficulty in finding other ways of communicating much the same thing. However, later I would come to question whether these alternatives were really paraphrases since I would come to understand the thematic importance of the choice of sentence subject.

In these ways then a teaching profile of my own began to emerge. A rather dramatic personality in the front, some silent periods, and some student discussion, all hopefully orchestrated around a series of text-task activities, in which the earlier ones paved the way for the latter.

50

Stories from the Sudan

In the 1970s the Sudanese were very likeable people; indeed, one of the few things that the Arab World at that time seemed to agree on was that the Sudanese were "naas Tayyibiin", or "fine folks". Despite their harsh environment and difficult living conditions, they retained dignity and a fine sense of humour. (Whether this has remained through later events, such as Islamicisation, the discovery of oil and the conflicts in Darfur, I do not know.) For example, they were very fond of their local saying, "When Allah made the Sudan, Allah laughed". So, this section consists of five stories, one from the memoirs of Babiker Bedri, two that I heard on more than one occasion, one concerning my colleague and friend, Phil Skeldon, and one from myself.

Babiker Bedri died in 1954 at the age of 94, a famous Sudanese educator, not least for having opened the first girls' school in the country in 1906. (His son, Yousef Bedri, was principal of the excellent Afhad University College for Women during my time in Khartoum, and was the co-translator of his father's memoirs, published by Oxford University Press.) As a young man, Babiker had been sent by the Mahdiist administration to a series of villages to collect a poll tax of two piastres a head. At a certain village, he had collected very little even though the village seemed quite populous. So, he came up with this strategy, which I tell in his own words:

I sat by myself in the street until a boy of about eight years old passed by. I called him and said, "Who is your father?"

"Abdullah al-Hajj 'Ali"

"What's your name?" "So-and-so"

"And your brothers and sisters?" "So-and-so and so-and-so and so-and-so".

And so we went on until the number of the household amounted to twenty-three people, whereas his father had only admitted to eight.

I let the child go, and after some time sent for his father and said, "Shaykh 'Abdullah, you are a rich man, praise be to God. But your fast will not be pleasing to God if you do not pay the tax in full. It only comes once a year, and the tax on your household is only forty-six piastres . . . Pay up, and clear your conscience".

"But", he replied, "eight persons at two piastres comes to sixteen" . . .

"Your household is twenty-three", I said.

"Never!" says he.

"You have sworn on the Koran", I said. "Well, then, listen to this"—and I read him the names of the people I had got from his son.

He thought for a bit, then said, "Who gave you those names?"

"So-and-so did", said I, mentioning one of his neighbours.

"Oh? And how many did he say his household was?"

"Five"

"Take your pen", he said, "and I'll tell you how many he really has".

"By names, please", said I, taking up my pen; and he gave me the names of fifteen persons.

I sent for this neighbor, and went through the same process, and read him the names of his dependents. He asked me who had given me the names, and I told him "Your neighbor so-and-so". He then asked me how many this neighbor had admitted to, and so it went on until I had the whole truth, and collected a sum from them such as Mukhtar had never hoped for.

The next story concerns the most famous Sudanese singer and bandleader of the 1940s, whose name I don't remember. The point of the story requires readers to know that the Sudanese colloquial Arabic word for daughter is *bit*, so *bit-Sadiiq* means "the daughter of" Sadiiq. Anyway, our singer and his band were sent as a present of the Sudan Government to play and sing at King Farouk's wedding at the Ras-at-Tin place in Alexandria. According to the Sudanese, the singer was a fine musician, but a simple man who could neither read nor write. Before the wedding, he was stuffed into a dinner jacket (aka tuxedo), and taken to some fancy cocktail party attended by the Cairo elite. At one point some elegant woman approached him and inquired, "Oh, master singer, what do you think of the music of Bithoven?" The singer, somewhat panicked by never having heard of this composer, apparently replied "Forget Bit-Hoven, I am a better musician than Hoven himself".

At the Faculty of Law, there were quite a number of very tall Dinka students, who told me this story. (The Dinka are not only very tall and very thin, but they are also jet black in pigment—indeed they claim that, as a result, their skin takes on a green sheen.) Anyway, a party of four Dinka were in London on some official mission when one of the party became separated from the others. So, after a fruitless search for the missing member, the remaining trio go to the West End Central police station and report to the desk sergeant that they have lost their friend. Something like this conversation ensues:

Sergeant: So, could you describe your friend to me?
Dinka: Yes, certainly; he is about seven feet tall, about a foot wide, and he is green.
Sergeant (making notes, "7' tall, 1' wide; green"): Well, gentlemen, given your description I don't fink we'll 'ave much trouble in locating your friend.

Next to Phil Skeldon, who is a tall, large, strongly built man. One day, he was awoken late at night to find a naked, greased dark Sudanese trying to remove his record player through the window. Phil, who slept naked, leapt up; the thief dropped the record-player and scurried outside with Phil in hot pursuit. The thief ran down the street, and seeing Phil catching him up, dashed into a passing garden. This was part of the official residence of the Tanzanian ambassador, who was entertaining outside various members of the diplomatic corps to a late dinner. The two naked men ran across the terrace and round the garden a couple of times, before the thief escaped down the street. As a result, the ambassador took a shine to Phil, probably because the "naked men" episode contributed much to the success of the evening. So when Phil told the ambassador that he was a keen member of Khartoum cricket club, the ambassador used to arrive with his two wives with a lavish tea for all the players between the two innings.

And my own contribution: In 1976, there was a so-called Libyan invasion and attempted coup, though in fact it is likely that, while Libya provided the money to try and overthrow President Numeiri, Chaddi mercenaries actually undertook the attempt. Anyway, one day there was fighting in the centre of the city as my sons and I drove into downtown, and I hurriedly turned around when we heard the shooting. A 48-hour curfew was imposed as President Numeiri rallied his forces. After the curfew was temporarily released I went down to my local shop on the corner of the next street to buy staples like bread and *foul* (the local beans). The local shopkeeper, an elderly devout Muslim, had always been appalled to learn that I was an atheist. So, as I came round the corner, he rushed out, saying in Arabic, "Dr John, you must believe". I inquired why and he explained that the only mortar shell in our area had landed on the house of the First Secretary of the Libyan embassy, causing a beam to fall and break his leg. So, he said, "Now you must believe in Allah; it is proved". Summoning up one of the smartest classical Arabic expressions I ever learnt, I replied, "I will take it under consideration". Every time later I went round for basic purchases, he asked, "Still under consideration?" and I replied, "Yes, still under consideration". He was I think sadly disappointed that I had under-responded to what he felt had been a conclusive divine portent.

51

ESPMENA Bulletin

After a year or so, I was well settled in with my teaching (including a course per year on applied linguistics for the Department of English), busy with various ESP curriculum development projects, and basically done with the "participles" working paper. So, one staff meeting, I suggested we should start a small journal, which soon became known as "ESPMENA Bulletin", the opening acronym standing for *English for Specific Purposes in the Middle East and North Africa*. (Although its meaning was clear, its pronunciation was often not—should there be an epithentic vowel between the *p* and the *m*?) I can perhaps best tell the story of this venture by quoting from two pieces especially written for the Tenth Anniversary Issue in 1985 (Bulletin No.20), one by me and the other by Angele Tadros, the editor at that time.

ESPMENA Bulletin 1 appeared in April 1975. Like all the early issues, it was duplicated on foolscap paper—a size of paper now unfortunately difficult to find in sophisticated places, so photocopying has become a problem. However, unlike the following issue, No. 1 had no colourful logo (designed by my ex-wife Valerie). Further, most of the first issue was typed on stencil by myself using an old but faithful Olympia Portable, whilst the Appendix was typed by the author, Ian Pearson. My name appeared on the top of the Contents page as Editor; below it was that of Gillian Hashim as Secretary. My name would disappear after a few years, but Gillian's has remained as Secretary for all the eighteen issues so far produced. Gillian Hashim is thus the largely unsung heroine of the ESPMENA story; from No. 2, she has done all the typing, maintained the subscription and correspondence files, helped issues through the labyrinthine procedures of the Khartoum University Press, and laboriously addressed and dispatched. Editors have come and gone, but the Secretary has endured—and much of the credit for ESPMENA's survival into its second decade belongs to Gillian Hashim.

The first issue was only fifteen pages long and had a print run (to use a distinctly aggrandizing expression) of only 140 copies. The copies were rolled up and stuck with Scotch tape in the early ESPMENA manner. It was the ragged consequences of this elementary delivery system that caused Gerhard Nickel to remark that ESPMENA used to arrive in Frankfurt looking as though it were entering the terminal stages of a "pass the parcel" game. I continued:

The warm initial response to ESPMENA much strengthened my application for support to the Ford Foundation's Linguistics Advisor for the Middle East, Dick Tucker, now Director of Center for Applied Linguistics, Georgetown University. We (Jim Crofts being co-editor at the time) wanted ESPMENA to be free of charge for as long as possible. . . . The $1000 grant was largely used for covering mailing costs of the early issues and later we subsequently received some funding from the Hornby Trust and the University of Khartoum Faculty of Arts Research Board.

And this from Angele:

> Four main sections feature in the later issues. These are: Teaching and Learning Materials, Articles and/or Research, Book Reviews and Short Notices. . . . As ESPMENA developed, the scope of the Teaching and Learning Materials section widened, and instead of the short exercises, more lengthy papers have been introduced with an orientation to non-linguistic aspects of importance to specific groups of learners. We thus encounter titles such as 'Towards an Integrated Approach to Teaching English and Mathematics (Issue 2), 'The Use of Role and Cue Cards to Practise Transmediation and Recording' (Issue 15), 'Materials for Law Students: Learning to Use the Library' (Number 17), or 'How to Locate Information: Medical Journals' (Number 12).

Re-reading some of these issues today, I am struck by the self-confident, pioneering, perhaps even brash, tone of the pieces emanating from ELSU. We certainly gave a strong impression that we knew what we were doing! Nor were we any respecter of persons when it came to book reviews. Here is the opening to Tony Bex's review of a book by a person already mentioned in this chapter:

> Peter Strevens' new book is something of a disappointment. Basically it is a collection of essays and lectures which have been given a spurious coherence by being placed within the covers of a single book. In his introduction, Strevens claims that in the past decade 'there have emerged a number of important issues and concerns in applied linguistics, language teaching methodology and the teaching of English, whose combined effect has been to open new paths of thought, action and development in the teaching of English' and that the book 'reflects these new orientations'. Unfortunately, *New Orientations* is not quite the survey that the introduction suggests.

ESPMENA Bulletin continued until the early 1990s, often being edited by Stephen Andrews, who had been at Khartoum Polytechnic before taking up a lectureship at the University of Reading. The last issue I saw was Bulletin No. 29 in late 1991. It presumably died because of the policies adopted at that time to Islamicize and Arabicize the University. Indeed, a recent search of the official website of the University of Khartoum failed to produce any mention of an entity that I had known so well and had always known as the "English Language Servicing Unit".

52

The University of Khartoum and its denizens

The member of the central administration I got to know best was the University Secretary, Mohammed Omer Bashir, known universally as *emm oh bee*. He was a dynamic and charismatic individual, skilled in getting the creaky administrative wheels of the university to move. Some time after I left, he was awarded an honorary doctorate by a British university. However, on arrival at Heathrow on his way to collect this deserved honour, he was detained by the immigration authorities because his name was on one of those notorious "watch lists", apparently as a result of his role in agitating for Sudan's independence some 25 years earlier. Despite the frantic efforts of several high-ranking British academics, M.O.B. was shipped straight back to Khartoum on one of the next flights—to the continuing shame of Her Majesty's Government.

The other senior official I had most to do with was Professor Yusuf Fadl Hassan, at that time the Dean of the Faculty of Arts, and also the long-serving Director of the Institute for African and Asian Studies (IAAS), the university's major research centre. There were particularly close relations between the IAAS and the Ford Foundation, as represented during my five years in Khartoum by Richard Tucker (later of the Center for Applied Linguistics in Washington, DC) and then by Bjorn Jernudd (later of the Baptist University in Hong Kong). Yusuf chaired the faculty Research Board, where I was struck by the contrast between the U of K's attitude toward research and the one that I had found at the University of Libya. For example, a colleague in Tripoli had been prevented from doing research in Libyan dialectology "because it might undermine national unity". In Khartoum, such sociolinguistic ambitions would have been firmly encouraged rather than firmly discouraged. Indeed, during my years on the board, I can remember only two proposals where issues of sensitivity arose. First, a proposal to study a language on the borders of Sudan and Eritrea was turned back because of the presence of *shifta*, or the nomadic bandits in that region. Our concerns had been reinforced by a recent event that had galvanized the city. The Italian ambassador, after visiting the ex-Italian colonial city of Asmara, had decided to return to Khartoum overland, setting off in a small convoy of three landrovers with diplomatic flags flying. However, when they finally arrived at the Sudanese border town of Kassala, the ambassador and his entourage were wearing nothing but their underpants. They had been robbed of nearly all their removable possessions by the *shifta*.

The other case that led to much discussion was a proposal by an American sociologist to study trade union opposition to the President of the Republic, Major-General Jaafer Al-Numeiri. Yusuf decided that the President's office would need to be contacted about this because of the likely political sensitivities involved in a relatively benevolent but nevertheless autocratic regime. Back came the response from the presidential advisors. The sociologist would not be permitted to study trade union opposition at the present time, because that activity might itself inflame the current situation, but he was welcome to study such opposition five years ago. An instance of Solomonic judgement, we thought.

In the seventies, the U of K was very much an elite institution with keen competition for admission. (About 15 percent of the student population was female.) Most of the students lived in dormitories, where they were also provided with meals. However, they had little ready money, and a group of four or five young men would collectively buy a single cigarette to share along with their morning glasses of tea from one of the tea stands on campus. Interestingly though, they always bought an expensive imported Benson and Hedges from its fancy gold box rather than one of the cheaper local brands. The students also had the habit of collecting long thin strips of paper from the dumpster outside the university press; these were the trimmings from the proofs, and served as a free source of note-paper. On these, they would write in truncated note form summaries of their textbooks, learn what they had written by heart, and then leave them on the unoccupied classroom floor. In time, I amassed quite a collection of these, something that I would later write about, as part of a chapter co-authored with Tony Dudley-Evans.

I became curious about the ways the students went about their university life, and the Dean of Students and I approached the Ford Foundation for a grant to appoint a research fellow to investigate student study habits. We obtained the then-princely sum of $40,000 dollars and appointed Dr Dan Douglas for a two-year term. He produced a book-length locally printed report, one key finding being that student study life was largely organized by and through the five daily prayer sessions. This discovery explained much about the student behavior, such as their readiness for classes at seven in the morning. Dan would later become a Professor at Iowa State University and produce the major volume on ESP language testing.

53

Curricular developments

There were lots of imaginative ideas floating around ELSU in the 1970s. One example would be Jim Crofts' work with the second-year history students. He went to the Department of History and essentially said, "What could I do in my English classes that would help you?" They said that in their major survey course on the history of the Middle East, they didn't have time for all the historical geography that the students needed to know—how the geography and the geographical names changed as successive empires came and went. "Fine", said Jim, "let me help fill in these gaps in their knowledge for you". And so he did; indeed, he wrote an interesting account of this curricular development in the EAP collection edited by Selinker, Trimble and Hanzeli and published in the USA in 1981. (This collection also carried a slightly revised version of my "participles" working paper.)

Paul Fanning and I developed courses for the Institute of Medical Laboratory Technology, which was part of the medical school. The students here were typically older and more mature; indeed, many of them also worked part-time in the various labs around the city, especially testing for prevalent diseases such as malaria and schistosomiasis. In the first year we used Joan Maclean's *English in Basic Medical Science*, as well as developed some supplementary materials. Towards the end of the year, I didn't want to give the trainees a typical student-type final exam, so I came up with the idea of compiling an index for the textbook in the last weeks of classes. It would, I thought, be an interesting way of consolidating the material we had been working through. The 17 participants compiled an alphabetical list of 130 entries, which I typed up. I sent a copy to Joan Maclean, who graciously thanked me and said if a second edition was in the offing, she would include our index. When I shared this letter with the trainees, they were both gratified and excited.

After four years working on our materials, Paul and I persuaded Van Milne of Thomas Nelson to publish a short textbook entitled *English in the Medical Laboratory*. (I think Van probably did this as a favour to me, given the success of *WSE*, but, in fact, around 6,000 copies would eventually be sold before Thomas Nelson was taken over.)

Here is a small part of the opening section entitled *Handling Liquids*:

Read

Accidents with Liquids [some drawings not shown here]

Sometimes specimens are spilled in the laboratory. If this happens, quickly take a piece of cotton-wool, dip it in antiseptic and wipe up every drop carefully. Burn the cotton-wool afterwards and wash your hands.

If an acid splashes into the eye, keep calm. Wash the eye with water from a wash-bottle and bathe it in an eyebath with a 5% solution of sodium carbonate. Then wipe up any other drops of acid from the bench.

Here is a NUMBERED LIST of instructions from the second paragraph:

ACID IN THE EYE

 1 Keep calm
 2 Wash in water
 3 Bathe in an eyebath
 4 Wipe up any other drops

Exercise 1

How many instructions are given in the first paragraph?
Write out a similar numbered list in your notebook.

As part of the short introduction to the 100-page textbook, we wrote:

We are aware that some of the apparatus and techniques we have chosen for illustration and practice have been superseded in the most medically advanced countries. We have preferred to use these simpler techniques rather than describe the operation of, say, the Electron Microscope, because we have had the requirements of students and trainees in the developing countries particularly in mind.

In consequence of this decision, the reader might not be entirely surprised to learn that a few years later the publisher forwarded a letter to me from a registrar at a major London hospital. The registrar argued that, since a technique we had illustrated had recently been banned in Britain as being dangerous, all copies of *English in the Medical Laboratory* should be withdrawn and destroyed. Needless to say, I disregarded this injunction. I do believe it to be the case, however, that Paul and I have the dubious privilege of being the only people who have ever been accused of writing language teaching materials hazardous to human health.

A number of us worked at various times and in various ways on developing an English curriculum for the law students. The students were required to read collections of criminal law cases, and I used to read lots of these, trying to find ones suitable for exploitation in the English lessons. I noticed that most of the cases originated in rural areas, where the local magistrate was a colonial officer often with little legal training. Many of these were overturned by the Court of Appeals in Khartoum, which was staffed by professionally trained lawyers. The judges had a particular turn of phrase for announcing this, which I always imagined to be dripping with sarcasm. That phrase was, "My learned friend has misdirected himself".

I also analyzed legal definitions, contrasting their forms and functions with the scientific definitions I had studied earlier. Arnold, I and others also developed materials for helping the students to answer examination questions at the end of the year. The only legal exam question that I remember went like this, which had some resemblance to the philosophy questions I had to answer back in 1958:

> You steal a bicycle from the university cycle rack. On arriving home, you discover it is your own bicycle. What crime if any, have you committed?

This is, I believe, a question about *mens rea*, or a guilty mind, and I suspect the correct answer is "attempted theft".

By late 1977, I had written up my analyses and sample materials in the form of a longish article, and submitted it to the *International Review of Applied Linguistics* (or *IRAL*), the leading journal in the field at that time. For reasons that will soon become clear, I do not today remember the original title. Indeed, the story of this, my first submission to a major journal, is somewhat fraught. The editor, Gerhard Nickel, replied at the time, "It looks interesting, but there is a large backlog and it couldn't be published before 1981". So, in late 1980 (back in the UK), I inquire about the publication of my longish article in the coming year. The Associate Editor replies, "When we said it couldn't be published before 1981, this does not mean that it would be published in 1981". I write a somewhat intemperate letter to Nickel about what I consider to be something of a deceit. He, however, does not budge and closes, adding insult to injury in my view, by noting that the paper needs to be shortened by a third. Through gritted teeth, I revise, dividing the paper into two basic parts. The definitions part gets published in a small Austrian ESP journal called *Fachsprache*. The remainder eventually appears in summer 1982 in *IRAL*, not as a main article, but in smaller font under *Notes and Discussions*, as "The case of cases in English for academic legal purposes". As for the moral of the story, perhaps all of the below apply:

Half a loaf is better than none.
Two for the price of one.
Where is Sudan anyway?
Patience rewarded.

54

Departure from Sudan

By early 1978, I was doing relatively well, or so I thought. I had published two book chapters, one on writing *WSE*, and the other, a shorter one, entitled "A survey of ESP in the Middle East". The submission to *IRAL* had been sent off, and the textbook with Paul was in its final stages. My working "participles" paper had been circulated, and was about to be favourably commented on by Henry Widdowson himself. My involvement with ESPMENA meant that I had been in contact with practically all of the places in the world where ESP was thriving. This certainly included at that time the University of Kuwait, where I had fairly recently returned from my first official overseas invitation—as a two-week Visiting Professor no less. My relationship with the Ford Foundation had been successful, and I had even spoken a few times at the University Senate.

On the other hand, living in Khartoum was becoming increasingly difficult. The electricity supply was increasingly subject to black-outs and brown-outs, making evening teaching at the U of K an increasingly fraught experience. Petrol was becoming very hard to get, often involving hours of queueing; sugar, eggs and charcoal (needed to warm water for the children's baths in winter) were only available on occasion. My eldest child was finishing her elementary education at the excellent international school, and we thought that prospects for secondary education in the UK would be better. (Wrongly, as it turned out.) The marriage itself was rocky. Meanwhile the university was beginning to lose many of its best people; the very best were obtaining better paid positions in the U.S; many of the others were attracted to the higher salaries being offered by the emerging universities in oil-rich Arab states.

So, I applied for a senior lecturership at Aston University in Birmingham in the Language Studies Unit (LSU), the main role of which at the time was to provide intensive pre-sessional and lighter in-sessional EAP courses. I went to the selection day, where all six short-listed candidates met up for lunch before meeting for 45 minutes each with the Interview Board. This process totally freaked out the two otherwise formidable American candidates, who were used to a very different procedure. Anyway, I apparently did well enough, because when I phoned the chair of the selection committee that night (again a British custom at that time) from my brother's house in London, I learnt that I had got the job. So, I knew the result before flying back to Khartoum next day on Sudan Airways (known to its expatriate frequent flyers as "Sudden Scareways").

The final exit procedure was as gruelling as that from Libya, but by now I was accustomed to it. As a colleague in Philosophy remarked, "When doing final exit, 'as one door closes . . . another door closes'". Although Angele Tadros and Andreas Lambrou remained for several years in Khartoum, most of the others drifted away as working and living conditions deteriorated. Tony Bex would have a successful career as a discourse analyst at Canterbury University in the UK; Angele Tadros would write an important PhD thesis at Birmingham under John Sinclair and is still teaching at a venerable age as a Professor of English at a women's university in Saudi Arabia; Paul Fanning got a job at Middlesex Polytechnic, and Arnold Spencer at Preston technical School in

Lancashire. Phil worked at Aston for a time, but, as of two years ago, was teaching scientific English at a university in Oman and contemplating retirement. When last heard of, Ian Pearson was Director of Studies for a British council teaching operation in Barcelona. Of the others, I have no news, despite some Google searching on the web. I don't know what the colleagues I have mentioned in this paragraph might now think about working in ELSU during my time there, but, at least for me, as director of the unit, these were good times. In effect, as an academic I was slowly coming of age.

FIVE

The Rise and Fall of the Aston Group

55

A sudden change of pace

Approaching my 40th year, I found myself back in England, but this time in its Second City—that of Birmingham in the West Midlands. Suddenly, many things were different. In Sudan, we had survived for five years without a telephone, either in the office or at home. If we wanted to make an occasional phone call, we either went to the nearby Department of Geology or to a neighbor (respectively). At Aston, phones were everywhere and, in the pre-email era, everywhere in fairly constant use. Travel was much easier: in the UK, internal travel had nothing of that complex expeditionary quality it had in Africa; external travel in Europe merely meant getting on a plane, with none of that laborious business in Khartoum of getting an exit-and-re-entry visa every time you ventured outside the country's borders. In addition, I now reported to Dennis Ager, the Head of the Foreign Languages Department, an excellent administrator with a keen and enthusiastic entrepreneurial sense. Indeed, he had been able in part to create my tenured senior lecturer position because of successful contracts with the Libyan Government for year-long intensive ESP courses preparing Libyan students to enter British universities for science and engineering degrees.

Dennis Ager had also established a splendid group of contract lecturers: *primus inter pares* was Ray Williams, a specialist in EFL/ESP reading and one of the best colleagues I have ever had the privilege of working with; Meriel Bloor, a functional grammarian and discourse analyst; Sandy Urquhart, another reading specialist and discourse analyst; David Charles, a methodologist and an expert in oral skills, especially in business contexts; and David Hall, rather more of an ESP/EAP generalist. All too had overseas experience: among other appointments, Ray had taught in Zambia, Meriel in Botswana, Sandy in Saudi Arabia, David C. in Singapore, and David H. with Tony Dudley-Evans in Iran. The Aston Group would shortly be joined by David Wilson, who had co-written a number of textbooks in Finland, Jane Willis, a researcher put in charge of an R & D project in the exciting new technology of video, and, for a few years, by Phil Skeldon. There was also a permanent lecturer, Cathy Johns-Lewis, an expert in English speech and particularly its intonation, who had been organizing the university's EAP programme for a number of years. We were ready to go.

The official name of my new employer was The University of Aston in Birmingham; it had been upgraded from a College of Advanced Technology in 1966 and, subsequent to my time there, it would simplify its moniker to Aston University. This technological background gave it a non-traditional, forward-looking character, and there was a strong department of Applied Psychology, as well as an engaging group of people—whom I would later get to know—interested in the sociology of science. However, the innovative nature of this environment was perhaps most obvious in my home department of foreign languages, where Dennis Ager had set up degree programmes in French and German with none of the traditional emphases on literature or on the history of European languages. For example, if the Aston students were to read a work by Emile Zola, they would not do so as part of a study of the 19th-century naturalist novel, but for the documentary evidence it might provide about working class living conditions and cultural habits in 19th-century France. Additionally, there was a strong emphasis on translation skills, which allowed many graduates to get jobs in their chosen areas of specialization.

56

Evenings around the kitchen table with Tony

I stayed with my old Libyan friend, Tony Dudley-Evans, for several months while we went through the slow process of selling our house in Leeds and buying one in Birmingham. Tony was living at that time (being recently divorced) in a small terrace house in the unglamourous Birmingham suburb of Selly Oak with his older child, Adrian. Tony worked for the Overseas Educational Studies Unit at Birmingham and I for the Language Studies Unit at Aston. We soon discovered that we were offering some similar courses, one being Report Writing for Overseas Graduate Students. We evolved a strategy whereby we would jointly prepare teaching materials sitting around the kitchen table, go off to our respective institutions to teach them, and then compare notes on how they went when we met up later that evening over dinner.

Below is a fragment of the teaching materials we jointly developed. It was entitled Explanation of Error, and was designed to help international graduate students with the phraseology they might need to account for unexpected results, anomalies, discrepancies and the like. It begins with a short list of useful 'skeleton' phrases for achieving such accountings, as in:

This discrepancy may be due to . . . .
The difference between the two sets of the figures could be accounted for by . . .

Then this:

Here are some test-retest results (i.e. the same test was given again and all variables were the same except those listed below). Offer *guarded* explanations of the discrepancy.

Test (85% correct answers)	Re-test (62% correct answers)
a. given on Monday morning	a. given on Friday afternoon
b. 75 subjects	b. 15 subjects
c. administered by experimenter	c. administered by experimenter's secretary
d. examples gone through	d. examples not thought to be necessary

In fact, this class activity would cross the Atlantic and eventually morph into a Language Focus section in the *Academic Writing for Graduate Students* textbook, which was not published until 1994.

In 2001 I wrote (with Chris Feak) a piece for a *Festschrift* for Tony on the occasion of his early retirement from Birmingham University to undertake a remarkably successful second career as the major jazz impresario of the English Midlands. Here is a relevant paragraph:

> The Birmingham collaboration between Tony and John in 1978–79 was one between two comparatively experienced ESP/EAP materials writers, who in the 1980s would extend their repertoires into more academic and more research-oriented roles. The serendipity of a shared house offset the fact that they were working at different institutions. Each had colleagues who would further contribute to a positive and productive materials-writing environment, such as Ray Williams at Aston and Tim Johns at Birmingham. Over that kitchen table and of an evening, we could plan next week's materials, spark and improve ideas, kill off weak or stray enthusiasms, and cobble together collages of photocopies and handwritten manuscripts to take to our secretaries for typing up. Yes, we still did that.

Tim Johns was, I believe, the most creative ESP materials writer I ever knew; in personal meetings, at talks, and at conferences, he would typically respond to some description of materials, with comments like, "Pretty nice, but have you thought of doing it like this? . . . " Inevitably, adequate materials would be immediately transformed into superior ones. Later, Tim would be a pioneer in using computers in language teaching, particularly for his ideas about 'data driven learning', i.e. give the students a bunch of data, such as concordance lines or textual fragments, and ask *them* to try and work out the underlying grammatical rule. Even later, his *kibbitzer* website at Birmingham University would become deservedly famous.

57

A gender awakening

The origination of this change actually took place in my last months in Sudan. I used to spend some time in the hot afternoons in the university library, often while waiting to teach my 5.00 PM class. I used to leaf through a remarkable local journal called *Sudan Notes and Records*, an amalgam of local history, biology, archaeology and cultural anthropology. I used to wander the shelves, noting on occasion eccentricities in the cataloguing process. For instance the Modern European History section contained a slim paperback by the well-known British comic, Spike Milligan, presumably placed there because of its title—*Adolf Hitler and my part in his downfall*. One day, I picked up a relatively recent philosophy journal, only to be wholly taken aback by sentences such as, *If a nineteenth century philosopher wanted to tackle the tricky topic of causation, she would need to pay particular attention to the works of David Hume*. At this point, readers might like to remember that I had gone to an all-male high school, attended a 90 percent male university, and spent many years in the patriarchal societies of northeast Africa. Certainly I had been brought up within the convention (already noted in a previous chapter) that one of my early heroes, John Bright of Bahkt-er-Ruda, succinctly summed up as, "In English grammar, man embraces woman". Indeed, readers may also have noted that this convention would seem alive and well in some of the extracts from my earlier writings.

When I got to Birmingham, I was therefore somewhat unprepared for encountering a group of feminist colleagues. These included Meriel Bloor of the LSU itself, but also Janette Webb and her friend Rowena

Matthews from the social sciences. In fact, we used to ask Dr Webb, who was a lecturer in social psychology in the business school, to give lectures on the role of women in modern society to the EAP and pre-MBA students attending our summer presessional courses, many of whom at that time coming from the Middle East. I was pleased to see the other day that Jan Webb is now Professor of Sociology at the University of Edinburgh. Although I have probably not fully freed myself from my upbringing in this regard, I believe I have become considerably more even-handed in my approach to gender issues.

58

A travelling man

I had only been back in British circulation for a few weeks when the British Council asked me to visit and report on their newly established ESP teaching operations in Munich and Hamburg—these were the new "direct teaching" initiatives, whereby the council hoped to offset some of their in-country administrative expenses by offering high-quality classes of their own. As best I recollect, the Munich situation was relatively straightforward, but the Hamburg one was a nightmare. To start with, the council officer designated to pick me up at the airport forgot to do so, and I didn't know where to go or what to do. (Memo to self—in future, always find out which hotel you have been booked into.) The next day, I was able to ascertain the following: a) the new flashy courses in Business English were seriously under-recruiting; b) the London-appointed staff blamed the teachers for not following up on contacts with local businesses; and c) the teachers blamed the administrators for misjudging the market, pricing the courses too high, and treating them with a lack of professional respect. In joint meetings, the atmosphere was poisonously vindictive. However, I did manage to discover that at least part of the problem derived from the fact that, for many years, a number of excellent freelance Business English teachers had been operating in the city and had established good relations with most of the major employers. In effect, they had collared the market. In my report, I urged the council to recruit the most successful of these freelancers and employ her as a liaison officer, but I never heard whether they did so.

Next up, I was invited to teach a course on materials production in the summer of 1979 at the ESP Summer School at Oregon State University in Corvallis. The American West was a real eye-opener. I stayed for a couple of days in Seattle with my old college room-mate, William Dunlop, and then drove down to Corvallis with Louis and Mary Trimble. Louis was a key member of the so-called "Washington School" of English for Specific Purposes, the others being Larry Selinker, whom I had met briefly at the conference in Copenhagen, and John Lackstrom, who would be one of the other instructors at the Summer School. Corvallis struck me as a pristine place, with its wonderful pines, its beautiful river, and its charming white wooden houses; it also turned out to have better fish and chips than I had ever had in England! One day, a couple of men with a large amount of equipment arrived outside my dormitory to remove a large tree from the street. In an amazingly short time, the tree had been cut down, its branches fed into a chipper, and its roots ground into pieces by some amazing machine. In an hour or so, all had gone. This was (in 1979) productivity of a kind and on a scale that I had never seen in Europe.

I don't think my teaching on the ESP Summer School was particularly impressive, except perhaps for a lecture I gave on my old stamping ground of definitions. At least, one well-known practitioner in technical writing remarked afterwards, "Well, John, that was a fizzer". In it, I had, amongst other things, discussed a short passage I had found in some engineering textbook. It opened like this:

Metering Pumps

Metering pumps are positive displacement pumps, driven by constant speed electric motors. They are used where a constant rate of supply of liquid is required, irrespective of the pressure. The motor, therefore, should be of such a power that it is not appreciably retarded as the load increases. The delivery is varied by an adjustment on the pump itself. The metering pump is usually a plunger type pump (Fig. 5.22), incorporating one or more plungers and the delivery is varied by an adjustment of the length of the stroke. In some cases, the plungers are replaced by a flexible diaphragm (Fig. 5.5), whose movement can be regulated.

This is not the place to expatiate on how this beautiful six-sentence passage can be pedagogically exploited, although folks at Aston would joke whenever some issue of text selection came up "Well, John can always use Metering Pumps for that". Suffice it to say, it allowed me to iterate a metaphor I was fond of at that time: "Definitions are pegs from which descriptive garments are hung". It also was a splendid general-specific text—notice that the first four sentences are full generalizations, but the fifth is modified by *usually*, and the last further modified by *In some cases*.

In 1980 I was invited, through the British Council, to give the opening plenary at a conference organized by the Institute for the Development of English Language Teaching in Iraq (IDELTI) in Baghdad. This was my first plenary and my eventual title was the somewhat bland "Reflections on the Teaching of Reading in the Arab World". I opened with an anecdote told me by a British acquaintance in the Sudan. He was walking down a quiet and empty street one hot afternoon in one of Khartoum's more restive periods when a very small boy on a large bicycle (clearly his father's) came by and shouted at him, "Do your accounts, oh khawaja". (*Khawaja* was a somewhat ambiguous mode of address often used to refer to westerners in the Sudan at that time.) So, in my talk, as a *khawaja* I attempted to do my accounts with regard to teaching students to read English in the Arab World.

Baghdad in 1980 was a pretty interesting place. For example, I went on several evenings to a bar with a number of the conference organizers. The first thing they did on arrival was to order and have placed on the table in front of them all the beers that might be needed during the evening. They said they did this because there was always a strong chance that the bar would run out of beer before the evening was over, although I never saw any evidence for this. Another thing that happened on arrival was the appearance of a small boy who would take your shoes away and bring them back later, polished up to a high shine. This was a free bar service that I have never encountered elsewhere. I met another interesting custom on the day I went to the sprawling Baghdad bazaar, where I eventually found myself in the covered alley of the booksellers. Right down the end, I saw an elderly merchant with a stock of English language books. I wandered in and eventually selected a nice hardbound copy of Gilbert White's *Selbourne*, which had originally been a prize at the old Victoria College in Baghdad. (Victoria College had been set up by the British as a kind of "public school" for the sons of colonials and of selected Iraqi notables.) I went up and asked the bookseller "How much?" To my great surprise, he proceeded to weigh the book on a scale and said, "two dinars". When I asked him about this, he said that he couldn't read English and so had decided that his English books were really like potatoes; the more they weigh, the more they should cost. A pretty good system, I concluded, in the circumstances.

Over the next few years, I was invited to several other countries, but the only visits I will mention here are one to Chile over the 1981–82 Christmas vacation, and one a few months later I made to Cameroon. The flight to Santiago stopped in Buenos Aires on the way down, which caused some consternation among the British passengers, because the Argentinians had just been defeated by Mrs Thatcher in the Falklands war. Eventually, however, all were persuaded that they would be safe in the transit lounge. Chile at that time was a stronghold in ESP led by Jack Ewer and Guillermo La Torre (who had together published an important textbook), and supported by important ESP researchers and practitioners such as Maria Horzella and Ana Maria Harvey, the last of whom was still active when I revisited Chile in 2004. Tragically, Jack Ewer, whom I had regularly corresponded with from the Sudan and after, had recently died in a climbing accident in the Andes, and in fact his body was never found. So, one day I was taken to visit his widow and, after tea, I was shown into his study, which was left exactly as he had left it when he embarked on his final and fatal mountaineering adventure. I didn't know what to say as I looked at a draft of an interesting-looking research paper on his desk. I wanted to say, "Somebody should take this material, pull it into shape and publish it", but his widow was standing sorrowfully in the doorway, and I left without saying anything to disturb the gloomy Victorian reverence of the room. On my final night, at the end of the ESP conference, I was in my upstairs hotel room (which overlooked a small garden) at about eight in the evening, when I noticed that a number of the conference participants had gathered outside. Suddenly, two or three guitars started to play and the assembled crowd burst into some jaunty Chilean song. I was being serenaded! For the first, and last, time in my life. I didn't really know how to respond, so I stood on the balcony, clapping, smiling foolishly and waving.

Now to Cameroon. When I met the British Consulate official designated to meet me at Yaounde airport, he took me to his office, opened a drawer in his desk and said, "All the women here are available but you have to be careful, so take a handful of these", pointing to a drawer-full of condoms. I (of course) declined. Right at the end of my mission, there was an official final dinner arranged by that consulate official. The star item on the menu was crocodile ribs. Well, here I am reminded of an account I once read of how to simulate the experience of ocean yacht racing: Stand under a cold shower fully clothed and tear up five pound notes as fast as possible. So, if the reader wants to simulate Cameroonian crocodile ribs, here is the procedure: Go to the local supermarket and buy several turkey drumsticks (the larger, the older and the tougher the better); then boil them in fish soup for three hours.

59

Vijay Bhatia

I was in the Sudan when I first came across Vijay Bhatia's name. He was a junior lecturer in India at that time, where he had begun to teach legal English. I will let him tell the story, which I have taken from an autobiographical piece he published in 2001:

I had written a letter to Angele Tadros in the Sudan requesting her to send me a copy of her publication on the language of economics. Unfortunately, she had already left for Birmingham when the letter reached Khartoum. The letter was intercepted by John Swales, who was Director of the Language Studies Unit, and also had an interest in legal English. As I subsequently learnt from him, he was equally delighted to find another human being on this Earth, other than himself, who was interested in legal English. He immediately wrote back, sending me, not only the paper I had asked for, but also a few of his own, which were more centrally relevant to my interest.

So, fast-forwarding to 1979, Dennis Ager and I agreed that we had made enough money from our intensive EAP programmes to be able to fund a three-year research fellowship for a PhD student in the LSU. I rang Christopher Candlin, head of the very impressive linguistics department at Lancaster University, and inquired whether he had any outstanding students completing their M.A. this coming summer. "Ah", he said, "We do have this very bright Indian called Vijay Bhatia!"

Vijay, who was only a few years younger than the rest of us, joined the unit in the autumn of 1979, and fitted right in as a member of the group. He acted as my occasional research assistant on a couple of projects, and helped establish what soon became *The Aston ESP Collection*, an assembly of printed papers and manuscripts that proved particularly useful when we later established an MSc. in ESP. His doctoral thesis was a discourse analysis of the recent UK Housing Act, chosen because it was *supposed* to be written in such a way that renters and local housing officials would be able to comprehend it. On one memorable occasion, we went to the House of Commons to interview a gentleman with the title of Parliamentary Counsel, a lawyer who had been responsible for turning the government's political intent for housing reform into legislative prose. Vijay was able to interweave Mr Caldwell's observations about his textual intentions into his textual analysis with impressive effect. Three years later, Chris Candlin came down to Aston to act as external examiner for the just-completed doctoral thesis, and he and Vijay had a lively exchange of views and ideas over a two-hour period. (One of the oddities of the British system is that the advisor/supervisor is not supposed to speak at his or her student's *viva voce*, and indeed has even to ask permission to silently attend.) In the intervening period, Vijay and I had participated in a very interesting multi-disciplinary conference on language and the law at Oxford, where we met a number of sociologists, linguists and legal scholars interested in that relationship and, among other things, we published later a short article based on our study of complex legal prepositions such as *in accordance with* and *in pursuance of*.

Vijay was an impressive cricketer, and the LSU used to be able to enter a team of six for the university's winter indoor cricket competition. Phil Skeldon and David Charles were also useful cricketers, while the rest of us could at least produce enthusiasm. One year, we fought all the way through to the final, which found us confronting a bunch of very tough- and fit-looking Midland lads. (Nearly all the other teams consisted of undergraduates.) Some psychology seemed to be called for, and so as the two teams warmed up in each other's presence in the gym, we could be heard calling to each other, "Vijay, remember that century you scored for the State of Rajahstan; how many sixes were there?" or "David, let's see you use that tricky leg spin that used to tie the Aussies in knots in Singapore". The local lads were decidedly fazed by this chat about cricketing prowess on far-flung foreign fields and we cantered home to victory.

As some readers will know, Vijay Bhatia went on to very considerable academic success, finishing, close to retirement, as a professor at the City University of Hong Kong. His 1993 book, *Analysing Genre: Language Use in Professional Settings*, largely set the agenda over the next decade for ESP research and materials development in business and legal contexts. The last time I looked, its Google Scholar "hit count" was around 850—a very impressive total indeed. I am, of course, very pleased and gratified at the remarkable success of my first doctoral student, and I also note that one of his daughters, Aditi, with a doctorate in discourse analysis studies from Macquarie University in Australia, is apparently continuing the Bhatia tradition. As Vijay noted about his "democratic" Aston experience, "The most important aspect of this informal, relaxed and friendly approach to research supervision is that it encourages individual growth rather than dependence on the adviser, although it is true that for a conventional teacher there can be nothing more difficult than abdication of authority in student-teacher consultation". With a student of Vijay's caliber, no concern about 'abdication of authority' ever arose.

60

Writing, writing, writing

In 1979, I was asked to became a member of the editorial board of a brand-new official ESP journal being established by the American University in Washington, DC—a few years later the journal was taken over by Elsevier and became *The English for Specific Purposes Journal*. As I had been developing a talk about ESP textbooks, I decided to go for an article on the topic, which became in the following year, the first article in the first issue. In the opening pages, I discussed some of the difficulties as I saw them, summing up the concerns as follows:

> It therefore seems to me that several strands of contemporary thought and opinion have come together to establish a 'rejectionist front' *vis-à-vis* the ESP textbook, partly because such books undermine the professionalism of the instructor and by extension that of his department, partly because they cannot meet the elaborated inventories of requirements produced by needs analysis or by schemes of evaluation, partly because they are offered in a format ostensibly unsuitable for communicative language teaching, and partly because their educational effectiveness may have been reduced by marketing considerations. The standard solution to these difficulties with published materials is for each institution, organization, or training establishment to offer its own tailor-made programmes.

I then went on to argue that such programmes were not cost- or time-effective, proposing instead that ESP textbooks should be designed not as hermetically sealed packages, but sufficiently loose and open-ended to encourage and co-opt locally made additions. I then illustrated this by taking the case I knew of English for Academic Legal Purposes. Although my solution would turn out to be overly idealistic, I have long believed that the basic arguments were sound and strong. Unfortunately, *ESP: The Textbook Problem* largely went unnoticed. (I have just looked it up on Google Scholar, only to find a derisory eight citations, the last being in 2005; in other words, just three a decade!)

In those first Aston years, I went to a number of small, specialized conferences/seminars, and revised versions of the talks would tend to be published in an interesting series of small volumes with the general title of *ELT Documents* and published by the British Council. (As far as I am concerned, the 1980s was the golden age of the Council; later, the splendid cohort of applied linguistics specialists it had developed was largely dispersed to make way for the new 'marketing' boys.) The only piece I will illustrate here was co-written with Tony Dudley-Evans and was entitled "Study modes and students from the Middle East", with Tony reflecting on his experiences at the University of Tabriz and I on those at the University of Khartoum. After some opening demurrals about the dangers of generalization, we attempted the following broad historical perspective:

> The important and unresolved issue is whether the current differences between Middle East education and Western education are inevitably a difference in social, moral and ideological codes or whether they signify little more than a generation gap. In other words, should we interpret differences between Western and Middle Eastern educational practices as being the differing products of, on the one hand, an Islamicized Near Eastern educational milieu and, on the other, a secularized European or North American tradition, or should we conclude that modes or study and modes of expression commonly accepted and practiced in the Middle East are in a surprising number of ways similar to those existing in the West 50 years ago (the teacher as authority, a respect for the acquisition of facts, a style of writing in the tradition of 'belles lettres', etc.)? In effect, are we observing a contrast

between youth and maturity of educational institutions, or radically different conceptions of the function and execution of higher education?

Not bad for a couple of ESP practitioners and materials writers!

Several of these small UK-based conferences were organized by members of what was known at that time as SELMOUS, which stood for Special English Language Materials for Overseas University Students. After one of these conferences, a group of us were travelling homeward on the train when we decided we had to come up with a better name. For one thing the pronunciation of SELMOUS was problematic; was it 'sellmouse' or 'selmuss'? For another, its rodent-like connotation was not totally pleasing. So, we set to work and after a bit came up with the Association of Tutors and Lecturers in English for Overseas Students; fine we thought, until Ken James of Manchester observed that the acronym would likely be pronounced as "at a loss". Hardly the impression we wanted to give. A few years later, the approved acronym was eventually established as BALEAP, the British Association of Lecturers in English for Academic Purposes, which remains to this day. So, a murine association became a pastoral one.

61

Aspects of Article Introductions

After I had been at Aston for a couple of years, I asked Dennis Ager if I could have a term off from teaching. I said I wanted to analyse how research article writers set about describing previous research (DPR), explaining that the existing materials in this area were woefully inadequate, even though writing up previous research was known to be a problem for many overseas post-graduate students. He agreed, and also offered a small research grant of 600 pounds to pay for some occasional research assistance (Vijay Bhatia) and for one of the secretaries to type up any final product as overtime.

By this time, my wife and I were separated and I was living for a few months with my colleague, David Charles, in his Birmingham flat before buying a small place of my own. The corpus that Vijay and I put together consisted of 48 recent article-introductions "selected at random (although with two exceptions to be noted below) from" the hard sciences, the social sciences, and the biology/medical field (16 of each)." As I subsequently wrote:

> The random selection had two pre-conditions attached. First, only introductions that contained at least one reference to previous research were included as, after all, the DPR was the starting point for the exercise. We do not know exactly how many articles were excluded on this ground but we suspect it is small. Secondly, we did not accept articles (with one possible exception from Education) whose main purpose appeared to be to review the literature; we felt intuitively that such survey-articles would turn out to have a different structure—presumably reflecting their different communicative purpose—to those in which the DPR was in some way a springboard for the presentation of new research. Again exclusions were few.

It can now be revealed (as they say) that there was a third exclusion. In order to keep the introductions to a reasonable length (just a few hundred words), I eliminated introductions that went beyond two photocopied pages.

So, I set to work to analyse this pile of photo-copies, this time using David's dining room table. A first attempt was to divide references to previous research into those which were *substantive* and those which were *cosmetic*, but we found that this distinction was very hard to operationalize. Instead, I came up with an overtly linguistic three-way classification:

Strong Author-Orientation
(Mercerau and Feynmann [1956] investigated the case of a ferro-
   magnetic sphere.)

Weak Author-Orientation
(Local failure rates as high as 18% have been reported [Cantin et
   al., 1968].)

Subject Orientation
(Computerised tomography may be of value earlier [Kahn &
    Berger, 1979].)

Then I had a couple of epiphanies. The first came from re-re-reading
my collection of 48 introductions. It began to look as though the DPR
sections were embedded into a pretty regular and highly rhetorical pattern. This seemed to have four parts or "moves"; so I got out my set of
highlighters and chose a colour for each move and marked up the texts.
Voila! I entitled the final write-up as "A Possible Structure for a Major
Type of Article-Introduction". A simplified version looked like this:

The Four Moves
Move One: Establishing the Field (43 out of 48 texts)
Move Two: Summarizing Previous Research (48/48)
Move Three: Preparing for Present Research (40/48)
Move Four: Introducing Present Research (46/48)

Here are two quick extracts from the monograph chosen to say a little
more about Moves One and Three. Here for Move One is the opening I
quoted from an article in *Language*; my commentary follows.

1. INTRODUCTION. An elaborate system of marking social distance and
respect is found in the morphology of Nahuatl as spoken in communities of
the Malinche volcano area in the Mexican states of Tlaxcala and Puebla. The
complexity of the morphology involved, the semantic range of the elements, and variation in the system in use raise questions of considerable interest for our understanding of the form and function of such systems, both
in Nahuatl itself and in other languages.

I suggest that the opening factual statement is a 'turn-off' for the linguist
without any specialist interest in Nahuatl. Putting it facetiously, how could
one respond but by noting 'I must remember that next time I'm in the Malinche volcano area'? It is the second sentence that *establishes the field* by the
appeal contained in 'raise questions <u>of considerable interest</u> for our under-

standing of the form and function of such systems, both in Nahuatl itself and <u>in other languages</u>'.

And now for Move Three:

> Occasionally, as in 2.1, Move 3 is spelled out in considerable detail; usually, however, it is either clausal or sentential. The other extended Move 3 is 6.7:- It is interesting to note, though, that nearly all modern work (except for Liberman) has failed to consider . . . . Most studies . . . have been content to . . . . Little attempt is made to explain why particular stress configurations occur, and why other conceivable types are never actualized.

From that time on, I became interested in the negative and quasi-negative phraseology used to point up a "gap" in the previous research.

The other epiphany occurred in the serials library of Aston University. I happened, also in 1980, to be casually reading a review of a recent work about traditional Javanese customs by the great cultural anthropologist, Clifford Geertz. The reviewer several times mentioned the word *genre* in connection with cock-fighting rituals and the arrangements required for princely audiences and the like. Suddenly, I realized that the concept of *genre* was the one that I had sub-consciously been searching for over the previous year or two. The following two-part extract from the opening chapter of the monograph shows something of how I was able to make use of the concept:

> I believe it is important to recognize that this investigation is genre-based. By *genre,* I mean a more or less standardized communicative event with a goal or set of goals mutually understood by the participants in that event and occurring within a functional rather than a social or personal setting. . . . The importance I attach to the attribution of genre-specificity derives from my belief that it is only within *genres* that viable correlations between *cognitive, rhetorical* and *linguistic* features can be established, for it is only within *genres* that language is sufficiently conventionalized and the range of communicative purpose sufficiently narrow for us to hope to establish pedagogically-employable generalizations that will capture certain relationships between function and form.

This episode has been longer than many and has contained an unusual number of quoted extracts, but for good reasons. *Aspects* represents a sustained analytic and intellectual effort on my part, and might in other circumstances have represented the core of a PhD thesis. It also showed that I had become a genre analyst, and one with both theoretical and practical aspirations. Oddly, however, I never thought of trying to publish it in some form or other, even if I did produce two later book chapters that reflected part of the story. Instead, it saw the light in the spring of 1981 as a 95-page typed mimeograph (with a printed cover) subtitled "Aston ESP Research Reports No. 1". (The second was a shortened version of Vijay's thesis and the third—and perhaps final—report was written by Jane Willis and colleagues on the Video project.) We ran off perhaps 100 copies and distributed them locally and around the world. For several years thereafter, a further 50 were produced each year, half being given to the students on our new M.Sc. in Teaching ESP. I doubt if more than 400 were ever produced, but, to this day, it continues to live on as some kind of *samizdat* publication. The last time I checked its Google Scholar total, it was over 190 and the ISI count is also very respectable. I can't help wondering sometimes whether half the people who cite *Aspects of Article Introductions* have actually ever seen a copy, or are just following some kind of citational copycat tradition.

62

Incidents in the Language Studies Unit

We used to have quite a lot of visitors to the LSU, often visiting speakers or overseas ESP lecturers sponsored on tours by the British Council. As might be expected, we often took our visitors to lunch. One option was to take them to the main cafeteria in the Vauxhall Dining Centre. And here, we had slowly to learn not to say what we would normally say to campus colleagues, "Let's go to the VD centre for lunch". (In American parlance, "the STD Center"). We found that this apparent allusion to venereal disease would often cause alarm and consternation.

The other alternative was to go to the staff club on the top floor of the main building. Here the food and its service were provided by the students from the adjacent College of Food. It was therefore fancy (the menus were in French) and the meals were quite heavily subsidized. We had to be careful though not to take visitors there during the regular examination periods. The waiters and waitresses had every move scrutinized by their instructors walking around with marking sheets. Everybody became nervous, including those taking lunch; we muttered, under our breath, "Please don't spill the peas, or you will fail". Typically, the final year waitperson students were presented with a whole orange for dessert, which they had to peel for the diners, using only a knife and fork. We watched in growing agony as they mangled this difficult task, only successfully accomplished, in my experience, by 60-year-old Italian waiters.

My colleague and friend, David Wilson always seemed hard up for money, largely because he had a family to support back in Finland, where he had worked for many years. Anyway, he found lodgings in a bed-sit in a rooming house run by a woman who rejoiced in the strange name of Mrs Horneyblow. At one juncture, David and Mrs Honeyblow fell out and he decided the only solution was to live in his office for a while. So he requested a second filing cabinet, in which he stored his sleeping bag, pyjamas, toiletries, etc. The only problem was the security guards, who made their final rounds at about eleven at night and their first rounds at about seven in the morning. So David had to stay up ostensibly working at his desk until the 11.00 PM guard had been by: "Working late again Mr Wilson? Yes, I will be a few more minutes, and then let myself out". And then he had to get up early and clear away all his stuff before the first morning visit. Eventually he found other quarters, but when, after the event, I told Dennis Ager, he expressed considerable concern, rightly pointing out that if there had been a fire in the building during the night the university would have been liable.

Phil Skeldon was in charge of a programme we had developed with the Japanese Ministry of Education to provide summer courses for Japanese high school teachers of English. The first year, we had decided to blow the budget on a fancy official welcome dinner at the university conference centre (where the participants would be staying), for which we had invited a number of senior members of the university, including the Pro-Vice-Chancellor (the number two). To our dismay, we soon discovered that many of the Japanese teachers were totally unaccustomed to dealing with knives and forks, and were actually watching the Ministry-appointed group leader for guidance, who in turn was anxiously watching us. All went relatively well until the end of the meal. The dessert had been apple pie and custard, and when the coffee arrived, the group leader solemnly poured the custard into the coffee and naturally all the teachers followed suit, one by one round the large table. The Pro-Vice-Chancellor's eyes were out on stalks, and Phil and I became so totally overcome by this unexpected development that we had to retreat to the kitchen in hysterics. Chastened by this experience, Phil decided next year to blow the budget on taking the Japanese teachers to attend a Shakespeare play at Stratford. He decided to get front stall tickets because he rightly suspected they wouldn't understand too much of the dialogue. On the coach down, he gave strict instructions that any kind of recording was totally forbidden. However, when the lights went down and the play started, a series of tell-tale red lights appeared in the third row as the teachers activated the cassette recorders hidden in their raincoat pockets. The front-of-the house manager stopped the play and temporarily confiscated all the recorders (to Phil's great embarrassment). After that, we decided that "discretion was the better part of valour" and the Japanese teachers would be handled with a lower profile. Interestingly, the last time I met Phil (in 2004 on leave from his ESP position in Oman), he was planning to go to Japan for a 25th anniversary reunion of the teachers' course, such is the remarkable Japanese predeliction for get-togethers of this sort.

63

1981, 1982, 1983: Three big years

The 1981 year started off with the distribution of *Aspects* to a gratifying amount of positive response; even Sandy Urquhart, usually the most caustic and critical of my colleagues, was largely complimentary. In the meantime, Ray and Sandy were putting the LSU even further on the map by planning the launching and editing of a new scholarly journal entitled *Reading in a Foreign Language.* In the summer, I went to my second international Applied Linguistics Congress, this time in Lund, Sweden. What a difference five years makes! This time I had submitted an abstract based on the article-introduction work, which had been accepted. For my presentation, I had prepared a three-page handout, all 50 copies of which I had laboriously hand colour-coded with highlighters to indicate the four moves. I knew I had some good stuff and got through my allotted twenty minutes (with ten minutes for discussion) with a fair amount of pace and perhaps some little panache before a full room of around 40 people. In the discussion, I remember particularly an exchange with a woman, who afterwards I would learn was Betty Lou Dubois from New Mexico State University and whose work I was already familiar with, about whether case reports (which tended to use a rarity rather than a centrality argument to justify their publication) could be seen as "an exception that proves the rule". I also noted that Richard Tucker, now the Director of the Center for Applied Linguistics in Washington, but previously the Ford Foundation Middle East linguistics advisor, was in the audience. After my session was over, I approached him and thanked him for coming. He replied, "Well, John, I have always followed your career with considerable interest". Wow, I had a career! Even more, an important applied linguist in North America was actually following it!

Also in 1981, I was invited to teach on the English for Science and Technology Summer Institute to be held at the University of Michigan in Ann Arbor for a couple of weeks in August. The invitation had come from Leslie Olsen and Tom Huckin in the Technical Communication Program in the School of Engineering. As I emerged from customs at the Detroit airport Tom played "God Save the Queen" on a cassette tape-recorder; after we had stopped laughing about that, we drove to Ann Arbor in Leslie's amazing 1962 Cadillac Convertible. The University of Michigan was an impressive place and its buildings and its denizens exuded style, wealth and academic self-confidence. (Aston seemed small and shabby in contrast.) I don't remember anything memorable about my teaching, but I did hear some lectures by Dwight Stevenson and J. C. Mathis on their important contributions to what I soon learnt to call *audience analysis*, and parts of this I was able to incorporate in subsequent materials for teaching academic writing. I returned the following year for a second visit, during which Larry Selinker, the Director of the English Language Institute at Michigan, took me on an official visit to meet the Associate Dean for Long Range Planning (what an impressive title!) in the Literature, Science and Arts College, but at that time I never quite understood why he had arranged this.

After many months of preliminary work, particularly by Ray and Meriel, in the autumn of 1981, we welcomed the first intake on to our brand new M.Sc. in Teaching English for Specific Purposes, the first post-graduate course of its kind in the world. We had titled this foray into specialized teacher education a Masters in Science partly because this was in keeping with Aston's technological tradition, and partly because of our commitment to putting specialized language teaching on a scientific basis. As best I recollect, we required course participants to have had at least three years of ESL teaching experience, at least part of it in ESP contexts. The first cohort consisted of a handful of British students, plus about 15 from overseas, most funded by the British Council, which had proved—and would continue to prove—very supportive of our initiative. One early activity was to give class members some direct experience of investigations in a scientific lab, which we had arranged with the Department of Physics, where I had been teaching a special EAP course for their international graduate students. At the last moment, however, the lab director insisted that all our participants should turn up in white lab coats and safety glasses, a not inconsiderable expense that we hadn't anticipated.

Beyond my role as designated course tutor, I also offered one of the major lecture courses, which was entitled Functional Varieties of English, a kind of survey of what we knew about the features of major genres in academic, legal, business and medical universes of discourse.

Two smaller courses were one on research methodologies (as preparation for the upcoming thesis work in the third term) and an elective called Educational Administration in ESP Contexts. This latter was run as an elaborate case study set in the mythical developing country of Tefloonia. Each four-person team comprised the English department at the nation's polytechnic, who are called to the office of the Assistant Dean (played by me) to respond to three recent letters he had received. Here is the shortest of the three:

Teflomine

P.O.Box 6, Ewerville

(last week)

Assistant Dean (etc)

Dear Sir,

I have been led to understand that the Polytechnic is
capable of running English courses for special groups of
people, and I am therefore wondering if you can help us.
We are planning to send six young mining engineers to
Minnesota for postgraduate training, but we feel they need
further English before they depart in September. Could you
give us information on the following points:-

    a. duration of course

    b. venue

    c. costs

I look forward to an early reply.

Yours faithfully,

Lester Scholles Jnr
PERSONNEL DIRECTOR

In a 1983 article describing experiences with this elective, Hugh L'Estrange (one of the early participants) and I summed up the primary objectives in the following way.

> The aims of the course were to force each four-member team to react to simulated realities in a variety of ways.
>
> A. To respond to requests for courses by:
> (i) establishing good communications with the potential customers so that as much information as possible can be obtained, good rapport established, and hazards in precourse administration minimized;
> (ii) preparing a range of costings according to various sets of criteria;
> (iii) considering the redeployment of existing staff and, where necessary, engaging in the process of selecting additional staff;
> (iv) drawing up outline course proposals that would be comprehensible and acceptable to all parties.

Although I found the designing of the case study to be highly engaging, its actual administration of the simulation turned out to be overly complex. As we wrote:

> Our initial experiences in this aspect of ESP teacher training thus suggest that there remains a problem in distinguishing the Dr Jekyll of supportive course tutor from the Mr Hyde of "awkward" negotiator. It looks as though—partly as a result of the limited histrionic talent available—we need another member of staff (who would not have any role or roles to play) to act as advisor to all the teams during the progress of the case and take on responsibility of evaluating the performance of all the players.

Despite this caveat, it remains the case that struggling with the four responses listed under A above is a necessary, if largely unsung, part of ESP management. As we found during iterations of this course, and I

148

have often found in the "real world", there is a perhaps understandable tendency for ESP practitioners to retreat to what they know best, such as materials production, rather than to engage sufficiently with the other stakeholders in developing the proposed activity.

In 1982, we were given a substantial grant from Britain's Overseas Development Administration to work with Technical Teacher's Training Institute (TTTI) in Calcutta in producing a new technical English textbook for the eastern region's 75 polytechnics. After some alarums and excursions with regard to who was going to do what and when, in the end the first author of *Communication in English for Technical Students* was Ray Williams, Rabindranath Ray of the TTTI was second, and I came along as third author; others though, especially Meriel Bloor and Phil Skeldon, also made substantial contributions. Ray was responsible for the opening Reading Section, adapting several of the techniques he had pioneered in his excellent *Panorama* EAP reading text; several authors, including Mr Ray, put together the middle Grammar and Word-Formation sections, while I wrote most of the closing Writing Section. I eventually structured the section around a top-down five sub-skills schema, which looked like this:

READERSHIP → ORGANIZATION → STYLE → FLOW → ACCURACY

So, in effect, first think about your audience, then about the structure of your text, and then about whether you would be better served by a formal or informal style. The idea of "flow" I got from David Charles, which he used to summarize as "how to get out of one sentence and into another"; and only in the final fifth stage should attention be paid to such matters as spelling and grammatical agreement. A modified version of this schema I would take to Michigan and would subsequently form a major part of the opening unit of *Academic Writing for Graduate Students*.

The 216-page textbook was published in 1984, just on schedule, and was accompanied by a teachers' manual. It was produced cheaply and in considerable numbers by the well-known Indian firm of Orient Longman Limited. The last time I looked it was still in print. Both getting this contract and getting it done on time further added, I believe, to the LSU's growing reputation, and probably helped to persuade the British Council in 1983 to choose Aston for an Anglo-Spanish project entitled "Research into English-language reading and writing requirements of Spanish academic staff", in which we were linked with the University of Cordoba. Here, our lead investigators and facilitators were Tony Dudley-Evans' wife, Maggie Jo St. John, who knew Spanish and who had recently completed our M.Sc in TESP, and Meriel Bloor.

In 1982, I was given the sideways promotion of a move from Senior Lecturer to Reader, presumably as a result of my increased productivity. Although, in principle, a Reader was supposed to have only light administrative and teaching responsibilities so that he or she could concentrate on scholarly endeavours, this did not really apply in my case as I remained the M.Sc. course tutor and head of the English Section of the LSU. It was also a sideways move because the pay scales for Senior Lecturer and Reader were the same. However, one unique privilege that becoming a reader bestowed was the chance of naming your own title and, as might be expected, I chose "Reader in English for Specific Purposes". As far as I know, I was the first person to have such a title and, I believe, to date the only such person in the British academic establishment. (The reasons for this will have to wait for the final chapter.) The other reader in the Foreign Language Department was a short, chubby, twinkly gentleman who had some years earlier had chosen for himself the intriguing title of "Reader in the History of European Universities".

64

English for Specific Purposes in the Arab world

During these Aston years, I had not lost contact with the Arab world, especially as there were typically several Middle Eastern participants on the first iterations of our masters course. I felt, however, that the Arab work in ESP was as fissiparous as ever because there were few contacts between neighbouring Arab countries and many with U.S. and UK institutions, which were more inclined to offer sponsorships of various sorts. In effect, what had emerged was a centre-periphery model. After a year or so's unsuccessful agitation to try and persuade some institution in the region to offer a regional conference or institute, in a moment of perhaps ill-considered enthusiasm, I decided that Aston would have to be the venue. I asked Hassan Mustafa, then of Manchester University, to be the co-convenor and Anthony Crocker, a very intelligent British Council English Language Officer, to be the academic director. Below is the opening paragraph of the preface that Hassan and I wrote to the 300-page proceedings volume that we published locally in Aston in 1984:

> This volume contains a selection of papers from the Summer Institute on *English for Specific Purposes in the Arab World* held at the University of Aston from the seventh to the twentieth of August, 1983. The purpose of the institute was to bring together ESP practitioners from all over the Arab world to discuss many of the crucial issues relating to Service English work in the region. In the event, there were sixty participants, representing 13 Arab countries as well as western interest in the area, and over half of the participants made a presentation in one form or another. The Summer Institute represented, to all intents and purposes, the Third Regional ESP Conference, the second being held in Alexandria in 1978. It is very much to be hoped that a Fourth will take place—once again in the Arab world itself and before another five years have passed.

I think many more years have passed before any such conference has taken place—if indeed it ever has—and from the second half of the 1980s onwards, the Middle East began to lose its leading role in ESP work. Among those whose papers were published in the proceedings were several by those I have mentioned earlier in this memoir, such as Angele Tadros and El-Tayeb El-Hassan from the Sudan, Stephen Andrews, ex-Sudan and now at Reading, and Tony Dudley-Evans. One of the participants who did not present was at that time the Head of English at Bir Zeit University in the West Bank. This was Hanan Ashrawi, even then becoming a known political commentator on and spokesperson for Palestinian affairs, and who subsequently, of course, would become much better known.

Early in 1984, I was invited by the council to give the opening plenary at a conference on English language teaching held in Alexandria, Egypt. The other invitee (provided by the U.S. government) was to be Professor Ann Johns of San Diego State University, a person whom I had never met but whose ESP work, especially on business English, was known to me. So, I was sitting in the lobby of a hotel in the Cairo suburb of Heliopolis with two or three senior officers from the British Council, talking about ESP matters, and waiting for Dr Johns to arrive. We all thought, I believe, that we Brits really knew much more than the Americans about how to go about service English provision in the Arab world. However, when this vivacious and witty American woman arrived, we were soon disabused of our prejudices. It turned out that Ann had spent a year at the American University of Cairo and had acquired much insight into the Middle East. It also turned out that her pronunciation of Arabic was better than mine, even if I did have perhaps a larger vocabulary! The following day was a day off before taking the train to Alexandria for the conference, so Ann and I spent several hours exploring the tourist sites and mosques of old Cairo and discussing various academic matters. This was the beginning of a close collaboration, the development of which will be discussed in the next chapter.

65

Episodes in ESP: A Source and Reference Book on the Development of English for Science and Technology

By this time I had become interested in the short history of ESP, partly as a foundational part of my major M.Sc lecture course at Aston, and partly because I felt that important pioneering work might soon fall into oblivion. Indeed, the title of my talk at the Alexandria conference had been "The First Twenty Years of ESP", starting, as I have earlier described, with Charles Barber's 1960 chapter, "Some measurable characteristics of modern scientific prose". (I had given an earlier version at the MEXTESOL Annual Convention in Mexico a couple of months previously. After my presentation, the English Language Officer from the council congratulated me, saying, "Well done, John, I have never seen such a rapt and attentive audience at a plenary in Mexico". However, one of the local organizers responded, "Actually, I think most of the audience was surreptitiously looking at the photos in the free copies of *Newsweek* that we had put into everybody's conference packet". An ego-deflating but probably salutary reality check.)

In 1983, I had approached Pergamon Press in Oxford about a volume in their Language Teaching Methodology series to be entitled *Episodes in ESP*, and the editors responded by offering me a contract. The resulting volume was something of a hybrid. I had selected 15 episodes (eleven articles and four textbook extracts); so in this sense it might be thought of as an edited volume. On the other hand, each episode was considerably fleshed out with an introductory Setting; then the text itself was accompanied by an extensive Commentary; this in turn was followed by sections entitled Activities, Evaluation and Related Readings. In that sense, it could be considered an authored book.

The rationale for *Episodes* can be gleaned from these extracts from the Introduction:

> Although this volume is in no sense a history of ESP, I have deliberately set out to try and establish a historical perspective. One reason for this . . . is a wish to show something of the causes and effects that link the Episodes together. Another is my wish to demonstrate the value of pioneering contributions. My own experience of the ESP profession over a period of fifteen years or more is that the profession as a whole, and with all too few exceptions, operates within the 'here and now' of their actual teaching situation. . . . ESP practitioners tend not to look *across* to other ESP situations and to other ESP endeavours, whether similar or dissimilar to their own, to see what lessons might be learnt, what insights might be gained, or what useful short-cuts can be made. Nor do they often look *back* to previous work in their own departments or in others. My feeling is that such 'isolationist' at-

titudes can lead to duplication of effort and inefficient use of time, and my hope is that this volume will do something to persuade the profession that contributions from other places and times are at least potentially relevant to the 'here and now'.

The book was published in 1985 and the reviewers were largely kind, although several pointed out that my claim that I had provided an objective account of the first 20 years of ESP was, at least questionable—as indeed the above extract from the introduction might indicate. One wrote that "Swales' presence is pervasive and persistent", and another concluded "The new era in ESP can be viewed more as a vision of its author and much less as an extrapolation from the events that *Episodes* chronicles and in many ways illustrates". Unfortunately, the sector of Maxwell's publishing empire under which *Episodes* fell was sold a couple of years after publication and it was re-issued, with a new Preface, by the purchaser, Prentice-Hall International. I say "unfortunately" because I never managed to learn the conditions and restrictions under which the British-based Prentice-Hall International operated. One thing that did eventually become clear was that *Episodes* could not be sold in the United States. It languished and mysteriously went out of print some time in the 1990s. Eventual total sales amounted to some 3,000. Given what had happened to *Writing Scientific English* at Thomas Nelson and now with *Episodes* at Pergamon, I decided that any future book projects would be offered to respectable university presses, and not to commercial publishers, most of which seemed susceptible to takeovers, consolidations, and sell-offs.

66

The British Council's 50th Anniversary Conference

I was, to my surprise and gratification, invited to give the lead paper on the English for Specific Purposes theme at this grand affair scheduled for November 1984, to be presided over by Sir Randolph Quirk, and to be held in the beautiful Senate House building at the University of London. The audience was distinctly scary, consisting mainly of very well-known figures in English studies from around the world. I worked hard on my paper in the months leading up to the conference, trying to fashion a sophisticated position statement. I chose as the epigraph, a couple of sentences from the 1983 *Local Knowledge* volume by the anthropologist Clifford Geertz of Princeton, who was often praised for his elegant and striking writing style:

> To an ethnographer, sorting through the machinery of distant ideas, the shapes of knowledge are always ineluctably local, indivisible from their instruments and encasements. One may veil this fact with ecumenical rhetoric or blur it with strenuous theory, but one cannot really make it go away.

As Tony Dudley-Evans would later comment, at around this time I would become entranced by this writing style, and would make some uncertain attempts to copy it.

The title I eventually came up with for my talk was "ESP—The Heart of the Matter or the End of the Affair?" I opened (in the published version) like this:

> As readers will recognize, my title borrows from the works of one of our most distinguished novelists—and one whose career has itself spanned the half century of British Council activity in the field of English that we celebrate this week. I also hope the Greene-tinted question in the title announces a serious attempt at the original request 'to take a bold stand with regard to future developments'.

After considerable gestation, the title, epigraph and opening sentences had been crafted in this way because—in a moment of what I fondly believed to be inspiration—I had come up with a neat way of ending the presentation. Here then is the final paragraph:

In this paper I have drawn upon investigative, theoretical and pragmatic considerations to put forward a case for the downgrading of both textual matter and subject-specific matter. In compensation I have argued for 'local knowledge', for a renewal of connection with the textual environment, and for greater attention to the tasks that specialized environments require of their occupants. I have seen our aims as perceiving and then pedagogically mobilizing interactions between language use, learning purpose, professional sub-culture and prevailing educational style. I have tried, in at least one genre, to relate these interactions to wider geo-political and geo-linguistic issues, and to show how prudence and responsibility may require us to give greater attention to Research English and to the business of its creation. As for my title and its original disjunctive question, readers who have followed me so far will recognize that what I should have written was:

ESP—The End of the Matter but the Heart of the Affair

After the paper was published in the conference volume, I sent a photocopy to Professor Geertz, and received a polite note of appreciation in response. I think Tony would conclude that the above paragraph was quite decidedly Geertzian in both argument and style. In a review of the volume, David Wilkins expressed surprise that I had chosen to focus on "research English and the business of its creation". However, the inexorable rise of anglophonicity in scholarly circles in the quarter century since the conference celebrating the 50th anniversary of the British Council might suggest that I had in fact succeeded in anticipating the prevailing future direction of the EAP wind.

Shortly after the conference I received a note from Sir John Burgh, the Director-General of the British Council:

Dear Mr. Swales

I am writing to offer you my warmest thanks for all you did to make last week's conference, 'Progress in English

Studies' such a great success. Thank you for your
stimulating paper and for contributing so actively to the
debate. As you well know, the subject of English for
Specific Purposes is a matter of great importance to the
work of the British Council, and we are grateful for your
considerable personal contribution to this field. . . .

Yours sincerely

John Burgh

This was a very gratifying note to receive, even if it was presumably not
written by Sir John himself.

67

The axe falls

Meanwhile, by the end of 1983, a crisis was looming back at the Language Studies Unit, even though our various courses, projects and visits overseas had all been going well and had made us an internationally
recognized centre for ESP excellence. The background is as follows. The
University had suffered a financial crisis around 1981, partly because of
Thatcherite notions of accountability. As a senior colleague put it,
"From now on there have to be at least sixteen bums on seats in all our
classes". However, the main cause originated in the fact that the previous Vice-Chancellor had allowed student numbers to increase beyond
those authorized by the University Grants Committee, which largely
controlled the finances of British universities. The new V-C, who was
British but who had spent many years at Stanford University in California, thought he could surmount the deficit by appealing for funds to
Aston's thousands of alumni and alumnae. This strategy was a dismal

failure; clearly the English Midlands wasn't yet ready for American-style *alma mater* giving. He then announced that no contract lecturers would have their contracts extended beyond six years because to do so would give them *de facto* tenured permanency. The final piece of the puzzle is to recall that Dennis Ager had recruited an exceptional group of LSU contract lecturers in and around 1978.

Dennis and the other professor in the department had high hopes that they could successfully appeal to the V-C to make some exceptions, certainly at least for Ray Williams. They made an appointment, and in the end decided that it would be better if I did not accompany the appeal party. I waited anxiously in the LSU office. They returned to say that the V-C had certainly recognized Ray's contributions, but he had refused to make any exceptions to his non-renewal policy. The V-C had added that from now on he would take a keen interest in all future faculty appointments throughout the university and that he was only interested in applicants who had first-class degrees from Oxford and Cambridge and had PhDs, and he wasn't interested in applicants who merely met curricular needs. The LSU was traumatized. It looked as though most of the contract lecturers would have to look elsewhere for positions, and it also looked as though Dennis and I would lose control of any future appointments. And so it proved. Ray and Sandy went to the College of St Mark and St. John in the west of England, and Meriel to the nearby University of Warwick. (David Hall had left a couple of years earlier to take up an ESP specialist position in Malaysia.) Further, the Vice-Chancellor was set to appoint a theoretical phonetician (with *his* requisite qualifications), an excellent fellow but one we would have great difficulty in using on our masters course.

Although (as a permanent Reader) I was not personally or directly threatened by the V-C's policies, I soon became concerned about my own future in a Language Studies Unit of a different character and orientation, especially as the LSU would undergo a major internal and external review later that year. I can't remember now who first contacted whom, but I do remember a number of transatlantic phone conversations with Joan Morley, the Associate Professor in the English Language Institute at the University of Michigan, and a leading authority on ESL in the United States. In the spring of 1984, I also had an exchange of correspondence with Eric Rabkin, the Interim Director, who, *inter alia*, told me that the two-year experiment to form the Linguistics Department and the English Language Institute into a single unit was going to be abandoned because of the very different disciplinary cultures of the two entities; later, a waggish Michigan colleague likened this experiment to "Putting everybody into a cardboard box and banging loudly on the outside".

Joan and Eric also told me that the Interim Director would be returning to his home department at the end of the year and that, yes, they are looking for a new Director but this would only be a visiting position because the future of the Linguistics Department was uncertain. Anyway, I decided to apply and hastily put a CV together. Not too bad: Two textbooks, the *Aspects* monograph, and *Episodes* in press; nine articles and ten book chapters; eight plenaries; one doctoral degree supervised, and two in progress; and various external examiner positions plus other sundry kinds of stuff. I was invited to visit, and went to the University of Michigan in April of that year.

I was in Ann Arbor for two full working days. I gave two talks; the one in the ELI I can't recall, but for Linguistics I had prepared some material that I had recently been taking an interest in—studies of citations by sociologists of knowledge or by information scientists, a field that I had got to know through colleagues in the sociology of science at Aston. This Linguistics talk was called "Citation analysis and discourse analysis", and was an early attempt to pull these two fields together. I had also been given a fearsome schedule of individual appointments with senior people in both the institute and department, but (strangely) there was no mention on the schedule of a formal interview or appointments board. So, I went round the various offices and did my best to take an intelligent interest in the scholarly and pedagogical aspirations of the denizens of those offices. At the end of two long days, Eric Rabkin, the Interim Director of the ELI (who was also the acting head of Linguistics, and who had been the Associate Dean for Long-Range Planning on my earlier visit) commented, in our final meeting, "Well,

John, it would appear that you have been interviewing us, rather than us interviewing you". So that was what all those individual meetings were about! And perhaps that was why Larry Selinker had taken me to meet him in 1982!

Despite my cluelessness about the U.S. "search" process, I was offered in May a two-year contract as Acting Director of the ELI and Visiting Professor of Linguistics, starting in September. I now had a serious decision to make, even if Aston were to offer me a one-year unpaid leave of absence. The situation was further complicated by the fact that I would be leaving my children behind and by the fact I had *finally* obtained a full study leave for the second half of the year. I also knew that the situation at Michigan would not be an easy one, especially for an administrator with no prior American experience. However, when I reflected on all the excellent colleagues who were about to leave (only David Charles, Maggie Jo St. John and Jane Willis stayed on in part-time capacities), the thought of soldiering on with a partly unknown team, and in a period with a major and unsettling review looming, was dispiriting. As in Leeds in 1973, I decided that tenure could be a trap. I accepted Michigan's offer, agreeing to take up my duties on January 1, 1985.

SIX

Twenty and More Years in the American Midwest (and Elsewhere)

68

Hard landings

I arrived in Ann Arbor just a day or two before the end of 1984, in time to take up my dual appointment in the English Language Institute and the Department of Linguistics, and in time for the beginning of what is accurately described at the University of Michigan as the "Winter Term." The term had hardly begun when the chair of Linguistics called an extraordinary meeting of the department's faculty. The Department was being asked by the powerful Dean of Literature, Science and Arts, Peter Steiner (of whom more later), to, in effect, vote itself out of existence, so that a new Interdisciplinary Program could be instituted as a replacement. (I was soon made aware of the fact that one of the few ways that tenured faculty at Michigan could be removed from their posts was through the "discontinuance" of the unit in which they served; others, I think, were "extreme financial exigency" and "moral turpitude.") As might be expected, discussion was both extensive and heated, and one important senior professor kept on importuning the chair with "Mr. Chairman, can we put a cap on this discussion?" Eventually, a vote was taken—I didn't cast a vote as a newcomer and a visiting professor—and, by a narrow margin, the Linguistics Department decided to disband itself. "Ye Gods," I thought, "What have I let myself in for now?" Shades of the Scottish Parliament dissolving itself in 1706?

Shortly afterward, I was put on the Steering Committee for the new linguistics program and we all met one evening at the new director's house to discuss whom we should invite to join the program and whom we would not. Individual CVs, after short discussions, were placed in either "yes" or "no" piles. The whole thing struck me, a green outsider, as an exercise in unexpected judgmentalism. So this was the way a major research university worked! As it transpired, the reorganization was only partly successful. One major figure left for another university after a year or two and another, Pete Becker, had decided to take early retirement when he was not selected to lead the new program. On the other hand, a couple of people, perhaps unfairly described as "dead wood," were persuaded to leave, while one or two others were forced to retreat to some other part of the university where they also had a fractional appointment.

I had kept up my membership of the *Linguistic Society of America* during my Aston days, and I attended the LSA annual conference in New York at the first opportunity. Perhaps it was the effect of a very crowded hotel, or perhaps it was the effect of the big and notoriously adversarial city, but I found the conference an ugly affair. The time allotted to papers was some 10-12 minutes, and everybody spoke very fast on highly complex topics. The short discussion periods were singularly short of opening complimentary remarks, such as, "I enjoyed your paper, but . . . , " and the questions seemed mostly designed to score points off the speakers. Meanwhile, job interviews were taking place, and there were milling crowds of young hopefuls looking for assistant professor positions, while the more senior members stood around in small groups exchanging knowing remarks with each other and totally ignoring the aspirants. The atmosphere was very different from the applied linguistics and ESL conferences I had been attending and, to this day, I have never attended another LSA Annual Meeting.

Another shock came when I learned that at the University of Michigan, chairs and directors of units were expected to set the annual salary raises of their faculty and staff, perhaps aided by a small unit salary sub-committee, and always subject to the final approval of the requisite dean's office. And here readers should remember that in Africa salaries were set, often on fixed scales, by the senior administrations, while in England, salaries were collectively and nationally negotiated by the Association of University Teachers, our union. So, this was totally new, as were the instructions from Peter Steiner that salaries would be based entirely on "merit," and not at all on "cost of living" considerations, and that any chair or director who foolishly and wimpishly opted for the latter would be in danger of having her or his unit's whole salary program cancelled. Juggling the figures with my administrative assistant—later renamed "Key Administrator" as the university embarked on a program of fancifying staff titles—took up quite a part of the early summer. Although there may well be merit in this free market system, it did mean for many American faculty that take-home pay became deeply psychological. Rather than thinking of salary as something that paid the basic bills, leaving hopefully something left over for vacations, savings, and occasional major purchases such as a new car, it now became an issue of ego and self-worth. This was particularly so under the Freedom of Information Act, since a public university such as Michigan had to make available a document showing everybody's salaries. This was held somewhere in the main library, and used to be regularly consulted by some on a regular basis, although I never bothered to find out where it was. (Now, I believe, this information is available somewhere online.) For example, more than once in the following few years, individual members in the institute refused to serve on the salary sub-committee because they were too overwrought by the fact that so-and-so earned more money than he or she did.

A further aspect of this system was that the Deans' offices had to hold back certain moneys each year for "retention"; what this meant was that professors would apply for jobs elsewhere and, if they got them, go to the Dean's office and wave their offer letters to the appropriate dean and say, "Would you like to match that?" hoping thereby to increase their salary by several thousands of dollars a year. In a much-recounted incident, a professor once approached the redoubtable Dean Steiner with such an offer from The Ohio State University (Michigan's great rival at football and in other ways) and asked for a concomitant raise. Apparently, Dean Steiner replied, "I don't think so. I think it will improve the quality of both institutions if you accept this outside offer." One can imagine that the aspirant left the Dean's presence, at least metaphorically, on his hands and knees.

My first teaching at Michigan was with the top-level students in the ELI's Intensive Program (IP). The IP consisted at that time of six levels, each of eight weeks' duration, with the assumption that near-beginners at Level 1 could obtain by Level 6 sufficient scores in the TOEFL® or MELAB exams in order to enter degree programs of their choice. My class consisted of about ten students who were set on obtaining business degrees. So, I devised a set of project-based activities for groups of three or four, leading to final reports and presentations. One was to examine and report back on the ELI's current account expenditures (as Director, I could give them access to these); another was to investigate the efficiency of the university's internal mail system; and the third at this point in time remains vague but had something to do with the ELI library budget and expenditure. These projects were great fun and also quite revealing; on the current account side, I was horrified to learn that at least 40 percent of our budget was spent on paying the basic monthly service charges for the telephones in almost every office. On the campus mail side, our data (created by getting the students to place campus mail envelopes around the university in considerable numbers and in a wide range of places and at different times and seeing how long they took to come back to the ELI) was sufficiently interesting to invite the head of the university mail service to hear the students' final presentation, at which she expressed gracious interest in what they had found. So far, so good.

Later that first year, however, I co-taught the basic ESL methods course for the MA in teaching ESL housed in the Linguistics Program. At Aston, I had developed into a successful teacher at this level, using my 15 hours or so to get through a considerable body of material, pushing through the syllabus, but open to comments and questions as long as they were directly related to the material. This strategy proved a total disaster at Michigan, and I got the worst evaluations of my life, one participant writing anonymously in the Comments section, "I'm afraid, Professor Swales, you do not belong in an American classroom." I was, frankly, quite traumatized by this failure, and it took me some time to work out why. I eventually realized that the 40–45 hour span of Michigan three-credit courses was designed to allow considerable participant space for open-ended and free-floating discussion (at least at this level), and that, in my zeal to be impressively professional, I had been denying them what they considered to be their rightful privileges. Slowly, over the following series of semesters, I came to terms with the U.S. semester-long courses, and eventually managed to obtain the approbation of my class participants.

69

The English Language Institute

The institute wherein I was the incoming director had a famous history and a famous list of previous incumbents of my position. It had been founded in 1941, as the first institute of its kind in North America (or elsewhere for that matter) by Charles Fries, a professor of English, and whose large oil portrait adorned the walls of the director's office. Fries remained director until 1956, and during these fifteen years, established the premier role of Michigan's ELI in North American ESL, especially for its Intensive Program, its textbooks (e.g., The "Rainbow" series, published by the University of Michigan Press), its development of the MELAB and ECPE tests, and its summer activities in ESL teacher training. The cohering forces behind all this were Fries' pioneering efforts to base a description of contemporary American English on authentic data (such as recorded phone conversations) and "The Michigan Method." This was an oral approach that began with very intensive training—often through choral drills—in the phonological shapes of the English language, followed by equally intensive practice in the essentials of English sentence structure. Only after several months of this emphasis on oral habit formation were the students introduced to reading or writing activities. Although today Fries' curriculum looks strangely behaviorist, it was rigorously applied and was based on a clear set of "scientific" principles.

In the second half of the 1950s, the director was Fries' long-time colleague, Robert Lado, an internationally known specialist in both language testing and in contrastive analysis. (Contrastive analysis involved a comparison of the phonological and grammatical features of a mother tongue and a target language so that teachers of the latter could focus on areas of divergence; for example, many learners of English are known to have difficulty with the voiceless and voiced "th" sounds, as in *thin* and *this*, respectively.) The next long-serving director was Ian Catford (1964–1975), a brilliant teacher of phonetics from the Department of Linguistics, who maintained the ELI's vibrant tradition of research into language and language behavior. On his retirement, he gave a wonderful series of lectures about his academic life; for example, in the first one he recounted that when he was a teenager growing up in Scotland, he had gone to the annual meeting of the Scottish Academy of Arts and Sciences where he made, before the assembled luminaries, some critical comments about a current transcription system of that time called *Bell's Visible Speech*. In fact, Ian Catford was an accent-meister and, indeed, as a young man, he had been employed by the BBC to play various British regional accents on radio plays. Years later, in 2005, John Sinclair, an invited speaker at a corpus linguistics conference in Ann Arbor and then living in Italy, expressed a wish to visit his old University of Edinburgh linguistics colleague. So, John and I went to have tea with Ian and his wife Lottie in their retirement home on the other side of town. On the way back, John recounted that in those old Edinburgh University days people crossing campus would be looking nervously over their shoulders to see if Ian might be behind them. Ian apparently had the habit of walking behind two or more people deep in conversation and imitating exactly their particular ways of speaking.

I had long known that Ian Catford also had some interest in artificial languages such as Esperanto. So on a day in the 1990s when Ian and

Lottie were coming to dinner (along with others), I extracted from my collection of Hong Kong postal history an 1890 cover from Shanghai to Budapest because there was an inscription on the envelope in an obscure artificial language based on Slavic sources called Volapuk. So, at dinner, I produced the envelope, like a rabbit from a hat, and said to Ian, "What language is that?" "Oh," he immediately replied, "that's Volapuk," and then he added, with his disarming modesty, "Well, as it happens, I wrote the Encyclopedia Britannica entry for Volapuk." A story weirdly reminiscent of the one about Sir Maurice Bowra at Oxford!

After a couple of interim directors, the next person with a five-year term was Larry Selinker, whose name has already occurred in this memoir more than once. Larry was an expert in second language acquisition, and, among other things, was interested in using the IP students as kinds of laboratory subjects. Then came Eric Rabkin and then me. Although I felt that I had skills to offer the ELI and that, given the recent imbroglios, there were clearly some fences to mend, this was offset by the intimidating reputation of the ELI—and of the university as a whole—and by the fact this was a larger unit (some 25 people) than I had previously been responsible for. Nor did I anticipate what was to happen after I had been there a year or so.

70

Another ax falls

As I have intimated, the main activities of the ELI in 1985 were the Intensive Program on the teaching side and, on the testing side, a test of the English language ability of international students applying to North American universities called the MELAB (and similar to the better-known TOEFL® exam), and the ECPE Certificate of Proficiency (and similar to the better-known Cambridge Proficiency Certificate). The intensive program was struggling somewhat, partly because many other universities had set up IPs, often based on the Michigan model, and partly because of what was known as the "pre-admission issue." The ma-

167

jor student-sponsoring agencies, typically at that time the U.S. cultural attachés of OPEC countries, were increasingly insisting that they would only send students to some university's IP if that university would guarantee that students would have a place in one of its own degree programs once they had successfully completed their English language preparation. It was made very clear to us in the ELI that a highly selective institution like Michigan would never agree to this. In effect then, the ELI was not functioning as a preparatory college for the University of Michigan, but for other less-selective post-secondary institutions.

Meanwhile the university's English language support for its enrolled international students, particularly those in graduate programs, was spotty at best. Originally, this had been the responsibility of the Department of Linguistics, but they had used their courses to provide teaching assistant support for doctoral students in syntax and phonology and the like. These students/teaching assistants had little ESL preparation, and there was sufficient dissatisfaction with this offering that the head of international admissions in the graduate school was sending students who needed further ESL/EAP support to a private language school in town. Although my predecessor had managed to wrest the course away from linguistics to the ELI, the new ELI 170 course was still viewed with considerable suspicion by the administrators in the Rackham School of Graduate Studies. The final aspect of the 1985 scenario involved what was known at that time as "The foreign teaching assistant problem." Every so often, the President of the University and various deans would be deluged with angry letters or phone calls from parents complaining that their children had failed basic math or science courses because they had been taught by incomprehensible Asian teaching assistants. Although the TA was by no means always the real cause of the failure, at that time the oral English proficiency of many international assistants was indeed lamentably low. So, in 1983 the College of LSA had brought in Dr. Sarah Briggs to develop in the ELI a mandatory testing program for potential FTAs; however, less was being done to help those who failed the test.

Another FTA crisis emerged in late 1985/early 1986 and Dean Steiner and Senior Associate Dean Jack Meiland called me to a meeting.

168

Steiner said, "I don't understand, Professor Swales, why your institute spends all its time on helping strangers when we have so many of our own students who need help." Good point, Dean, very good point. Steiner and Meiland then went on to say that they wanted the Intensive Program closed down so that more resources could be devoted to enrolled students. Another ax falls.

71

An exercise in "re-missioning"

My senior colleagues and I attempted to negotiate a compromise position in which we would keep the top three levels of the year-round IP, but give up the lower three; however, the dean was adamant that he wanted a clean break with the historic past. There were several large and immediate problems to be tackled: We needed to avoid severe downsizing in the institute staff; we needed to get a new EAP curriculum developed and approved at the College level; we needed to persuade Rackham (the graduate school) and the other admitting units that we could deliver a professional and valuable educational product; and we needed to make sure that the teaching staff could make the transition from the old IP to the new EAP enrolled-student environment. Rather a tall order, I ruefully thought.

However, Steiner and Meiland were cognizant of the size of the task. Peter Steiner, in particular, explained that he wanted a professional operation to be largely run through well-trained lecturers, rather than TAs; that the classes could be relatively small; they could be labor-intensive because they would likely require materials created in-house; and that the ELI courses shouldn't carry such a high credit load that international students would have to drop some of their degree courses to meet their English language requirements. This was a vision well attuned to the educational realities of the situation, and I believe it was right then and remains correct to this day. In addition, it offered a strong foundation on which we could build.

On the staffing side, three older members of staff (the Assistant Director, who had looked after admissions, visas, student welfare and so on; a long-serving lecturer; and the Administrative Assistant) decided, on contemplating the upheavals to come, to take the option of early retirement. Further, Jack Meiland agreed that the Assistant Director line could be transferred to the Testing and Certification Division, creating a half-time post for TA testing and a half-time post for re-evaluating the English of those incoming international students who had not taken English language first degrees. I then spent many an anxious night juggling around sets of courses and activities in such a way that all remaining members of the institute could keep their jobs. This effort resulted in an elaborate series of flip-chart sheets showing that if we did this, that, and the other, everything and everybody would be all right. I presented all this at a key staff meeting, after which one participant commented, "I thought, on several occasions, that your house of cards was about to collapse, but somehow it didn't."

For a start, we developed a suite of six 20-hour one-credit courses—Academic Writing, Academic Reading and Vocabulary, Lecture Comprehension, Academic Speaking, and Pronunciation I (speech sounds) and Pronunciation II (stress and intonation). Carolyn Madden (who has a section to herself in my *Other Floors, Other Voices* book) became course coordinator, Professor Joan Morley took charge of the pronunciation courses, I took on the Academic Writing, and lecturers were responsible for the materials development of the rest. A major stroke of luck was that Assistant Professor Sue Gass (of the ELI and Linguistics) was at that time on the college curriculum committee, where she successfully argued that the language level of these courses was equivalent to 300-level courses in European languages and so they should have 300 numbers. This was a splendid development because graduate students were much more accepting of courses thus enumerated than the 100 (entering undergraduate) numbers that unfortunately prevail across so much of U.S. EAP landscape.

We also made progress in persuading the admitting officers that we meant serious business, although the School of Public Health continued to send its international master's students to the private language school for a number of years. With Peter Steiner's enthusiastic support, we obtained a grant from the Center for Research on Learning and Teaching to develop materials for international teaching assistants; my research assistant, who was writing her dissertation on the discourse of undergraduate math classes, and I developed a 60-page workbook called *College Classroom Discourse* along with an accompanying videotape. Meanwhile, my fears that the teaching staff would not transition well from a comfy IP teaching environment to the demands of a hard-driving, every minute counts, atmosphere for classes that would only meet once a week for 90 minutes were largely unfounded. Although there were some initial anxieties and grumblings, that wonderful American capacity to be resilient in the face of radical change won through. We had successfully restructured and survived.

I do not intend to spend much space in the rest of this chapter on subsequent curricular developments, having preferred to concentrate on the radical events of 1985–1986. After all, anybody interested can find much information about the current state of affairs on the ELI website. However, I should perhaps mention the following: The ELI now offers some 35 courses a year, including several courses that accrue graduate credit; the training of what are now called International Graduate Student Instructors is conducted through official semester-long courses, as well as three-week workshops; we have special summer pre-MBA and pre-law programs of high quality; we offer many well-attended workshops; and we have popular one-on-one speaking and writing clinics. Although, of course, there is always room for further improvement and for constant attention to changes in our target populations, there has been for many years a certain richness and flexibility to our activities that is reflected in the high teaching evaluations that ELI instructors typically receive. However, this richness and this flexibility in our offerings is tied to two things: First, we provide in effect a "longitudinal" syllabus whereby students can take a mini-course as and when an increased communicative demand arises throughout their time at Michigan; second, it is achievable by our anomalous set of short courses and by the consequent anomalous arrangements for lecturer teaching loads. As I write, once again there is discussion in the Dean's

Office as to whether the ELI needs to be brought administratively into line with the rest of the college. The old struggle between administrative standardization and educational creativity continues to rumble on.

72

The ESP Journal/English for Specific Purposes— An International Journal

In Episode 60, I discussed an article I wrote for the first issue of *The ESP Journal*, as it was then called. By 1984, the journal was falling behind schedule and the members of the Editorial Board, which included Ann Johns and myself, were becoming worried. I contacted Ann and we successfully approached the publisher, Pergamon, about becoming co-editors. Our first issue was 4:2, and below is the first paragraph of our first joint editorial:

> Readers may have noticed with this issue that there have been changes in the editorial staff of the Journal. About a year ago Grace Burkart, who has had prime editorial responsibility for *The ESP Journal* since its inception in 1980, decided that her other commitments precluded her giving the Journal the attention it requires. We, as the new editors, had hoped to produce issue 4:2 by the end of 1985; unfortunately, this did not prove to be possible, largely because of the number of parties involved in the transition (the Oxford and New York offices of Pergamon, the American University as copyright holders and two new editors). However, it remains our firm intention to get both issues of Volume 5 to subscribers by the end of the 1986 calendar year.

We did succeed in bringing the journal back on schedule, partly because in those early days we had to produce only two issues a year. However, getting the issues out was typically a struggle and a muddle. In those days, good quality manuscripts were not in abundant supply, although they did come from all quarters of the globe; what at one moment seemed to be feast of publishable stuff would suddenly turn into a famine; the processes were slower because of the preponderance of snail mail; and despite the frequent phone calls between San Diego and Ann Arbor, we sometimes found that we had been doing things twice. We would exchange photocopies of all incoming manuscripts and in principle agree which co-editor would be most suitable to manage the review and editorial process, but sometimes this agreement became lost in the pressure of other business, and we finished up double-editing the same accepted submission! We even managed to "lose" the occasional manuscript, and Ann remembers at a conference in Singapore hiding behind a tree to avoid an author who hadn't heard from us for months because his masterwork had somehow disappeared. By today's standards, we were a couple of willing amateurs, and were assisted by a stream of equally willing but equally amateurish student assistants.

We also enjoyed teasing each other about transatlantic proclivities. Phone conversations might go like this:

> *Ann:* I've got another of those British papers. There are lots of good ideas up front, but the data is small, the methodology is suspect, the results thin, and the so-called discussion is just a summary because all the interesting stuff is in the introduction.
>
> *John:* Well, I've got one of those American efforts. The intro is just a comprehensive listing of previous research, the methods part is overly detailed and stodgy, and the results are extensive but hard to interpret, only right toward the end of the discussion is there any intellectual spark when the author discusses possibilities for future research.

Rhetorical dances of different kinds are being performed here—a British quickstep as opposed to an American Viennese Waltz. However, today these differences have been much diminished and no longer is it so easy to tell where an anonymous manuscript comes from.

At the annual TESOL International convention, there was always a meeting of the journal editors in the field, where common issues and problems would be discussed. This could be highly educational for us as arcane discussions unfolded about the likes of page budgets, citational indexes, turnaround times, what to do about a totally destructive review, and the finer points of the American Psychological Association's style manual. One of these topics might be the submission of the same manuscript simultaneously to more than one journal. And here one year the editor of one of the top journals told this story. It turned out that the same manuscript had been submitted the same week to his journal and to another leading journal—they having discovered this by each editor choosing the same reviewer, who then called them up and said, "Hey, did you know that I have this week received the same submission from the two of you?" The editors then decided that they would jointly send a very firm letter to the miscreant basically saying that he or she should never darken their editorial doorsteps with a manuscript ever again; in effect, the author would be "blacklisted." "That would do it," they thought. However, the transgressing author replied, totally unabashed, with an argument along these lines: "I never thought I would get published in either of your famous and highly competitive journals, but I knew I would get such really excellent reviews from you that I could then revise my manuscript and get accepted by some lesser journal, so, you see, I never *really* submitted to you."

As the years passed, what had originally been great enthusiasm for our co-editing work slowly began to diminish, especially after we moved to three issues a year, and in the end running a journal increasingly seemed to be onerous and wearisome. Ann stepped down in 1993 and I followed in 1994. Here is a paragraph from my final editorial:

> A 9-year run as an editor is a sizeable chunk of a person's working lifetime and during this "long turn" I have accumulated many debts (and many files). I have already written in the Volume 12(2) "From the Editors" of my abiding appreciation of a long-running and vibrant partnership with Ann Johns. Since 1990, I have also enjoyed working with Tony [Dudley-Evans] and, more recently, with Liz [Hamp-Lyons], even if these relationships have also confirmed to me that it is time for the last of the "old guard" to make way for a somewhat younger, and certainly fresher, replacement. The new

team will doubtless be reconsidering some of those questions about journal policy that have occurred and recurred over the last decade. Should the journal continue with an "open" manuscript review process? Is it time to move to an increased annual page budget (doubtless accompanied by an increase in subscription)? Are special thematic or regional issues worth the disruption in manuscript flow and extra effort they seem to engender? Like you, I shall be watching this space for developments.

In fact, *English for Specific Purposes* did soon follow fashion and move to "blind review" and did move to four issues a year, as well as eventually entering the new age of electronic submission, review, and editorial work. However, Ann and I continue to appear on the masthead as "Editors Emeritus," some recognition for all those years of unpaid labor.

I did keep the "files" for several years since they consisted of original manuscripts, reviews, revisions, and editorial correspondence. These, I thought, would make a splendid source of data for a dissertation, but none of my students ever wanted to take it up. However, I did later publish a chapter on a collection of "submission letters" accompanying manuscripts sent to the journal. Some of these contained various idiosyncracies, such as, "Please make any changes that you consider necessary." The chapter's title was "Occluded Genres: The Case of the Submission Letter." I had thought up *occluded* as a way of getting at genres (such as reviews and recommendations) that are "out of sight" for all except a privileged few. The label has sort of stuck, although I sometimes think today, with all the information obtainable on the Internet or available through workshops and manuals, that *occluded genres* hardly exist in the academy anymore.

73

Working with doctoral students

During my Michigan years, I was regularly involved with graduate students; for example, I was a long-serving member of the Graduate Affairs Committee in Linguistics, often working closely with Pam Beddor (the chair) on monitoring doctoral students' progress, trying to make sure they received funding for tuition, helping them get grants of various kinds, and so on. I was chair or co-chair of about 20 dissertation committees during my time in Ann Arbor, the first two graduating in 1989, and often served as an outside member of committees, particularly for the School of Education. On the whole, I greatly enjoyed working with doctoral students, as well as with visiting scholars and senior undergraduates, and I certainly devoted quite a lot of time and effort to advising activities of one kind or another. (I always disliked and avoided the term *mentor* as being both superior-sounding and overly intrusive.) Typically, this advising consisted of individual meetings focused on the student's writing, reading, and thinking.

I did, however, have something of a brainwave early in the 1990s. At that time, I was advisor to four doctoral students in linguistics, which was quite a lot, given everything else. So, one day, I thought, "Why don't we all meet once a week as a group, rather than always having one-on-one meetings?" Thus the Doctoral Group was born, and would continue for many years with a changing cast of characters. Although belonging to a research group of some kind has today become *de rigeur* for doctoral students in Michigan's Department of Linguistics, some fifteen years ago it was, I believe, quite innovative, at least in the humanities. The original "quartet" have written up their experiences and so, in a move perhaps in keeping with my advising "philosophy," I will pass the baton over to them. Although their accounts are broadly laudatory, I have chosen three extracts that lean (delightfully) toward the "tongue-in-cheek":

> The main purpose of the weekly Doctoral Group meetings was for us to report on what we had done, or failed to do, the previous week, and make rash promises about what we would do in the week ahead. Each of us had a different approach to these reports; some believed that it was best to take a professional tack, while others felt that a few jokes at John's expense might help distract from the absence of progress to report (these differing styles may also be observed in the stories that follow).

The power relationship between students and advisors is such that ideas intended by the advisor to be presented as a "suggestion" may be interpreted by the student as a stronger directive, as an order. John tried very hard to walk the fine line between the two and was often, though not always, successful. He urged us to think about our long-term goals and about other choices, but the decisions were always *ours*. John accepted our decisions, even when they involved rejections of his suggestions, albeit grudgingly when he was convinced he was right.

Only when he really gets fed up will he rewrite a paragraph or two, the decipherment of which usually requires the work of two or three students. This relatively hands-off approach sometimes left me frustrated. I wanted him to rewrite my paragraphs, because at least then they would sound all right (if a trifle Swalesian). He did rewrite a few paragraphs of my prospectus, which I later incorporated into a chapter of the dissertation; upon reading the section where the paragraphs reappeared, he wrote in the margin (in green ink) "brilliant!" and also commented on their brilliance in conversation. Me, dryly: "You wrote that part." John, unperturbed: "Oh. Did I?"

The final stage of a doctoral student's career is the oral defense of his or her dissertation (apart from some final post-defense revisions to the document). In my earlier days at Michigan, I had attended a number of these, either as committee member or co-chair and I had become dissatisfied with the candidate's opening formal 20-minute synopsis of the study. One day, Pete Becker and I were talking about this and we concluded that it made for a more relaxed yet more intellectually engaging *conversazione* if, instead, the candidate offered a personal narrative of how she got into the topic, what she learned along the way, what she liked best, what she might do differently if starting again, etc. And so, this was a policy I adopted whenever circumstances permitted. I also learned something else from a dissertation defense chaired by Professor Stapp from the School of Natural Resources. I had been invited to participate as a substitute examiner (the German candidate had been taking my dissertation writing class and one of her regular committee members had fallen ill, so I was asked to step in since I was familiar with her work). It transpired that her parents had come from Germany to attend the defense, and right at the end, Professor Stapp, with an elderly twinkle in his eye, said, "Well, young woman, I am not going to give you your PhD until one of your parents asks a decent question, and you give a decent answer." And, indeed, this took place. Whenever possible, as chair, I later followed Stapp's lead, although I always gave the candidate due warning of my intention to ask for a last question from a member of his or her family. This final exchange provided, in my opinion, a neat sense of closure to the event.

74

The Directorship of the ELI

In the winter of 1986-1987 an international search for a new ELI Director was launched, and naturally enough I put in an application, and was eventually placed on a short-list of three candidates. As part of the grueling search process, the short-listed candidates had 30-minute meetings with the august Executive Committee of the College of Literature, Science, and the Arts. Early on in my meeting, one of the members inquired as to why I had become so interested in scientific English, rather than in other varieties more typical of the humanities. As best I recollect, I replied approximately as follows:

> My grandfather and father were both successful civil engineers. My father was perhaps unusual in that he had never read a novel in his life, believing that it was a waste of time to read something that was obviously untrue. So, as a teenager, I rebelled against what I privately thought was his philistine attitude, and became something of a pseudo-intellectual aesthete. Later on in life, I came round to appreciating science and engineering writing. So, in answer to your question, I guess the reason for my interest in this variety must be "my genetic inheritance."

This reply got a big laugh, and the rest of the meeting went smoothly.

On May 29, I received a letter from the Dean, the first and fourth paragraphs of which I reproduce here:

Dear John:

After a thorough search for a Director of the English Language Institute, we have confirmed what we strongly suspected at the beginning: we already have the best possible candidate on campus, serving as Acting Director. With the support of the College Executive Committee, and the Vice-President for Academic Affairs, I am pleased to offer you the position of Professor of Linguistics, with tenure. I am also offering you the post of Director of the English Language Institute for a five-year term, beginning in the 1987–1988 academic year.

I very much hope you will accept this offer. The past two years have been difficult, but important in the history of ELI. I believe that the Institute, under your leadership, will become a significant force both on this campus, and in the broader discipline of applied linguistics. I am confident that we have the opportunity to rebuild ELI's international reputation as a major center of teaching and research.

I accepted the offer, managing to obtain a semester of leave in the 1989–1990 year. In fact, I would eventually continue to remain as Director for many more years, not retiring from the position until 2001, with Joan Morley standing in as Acting Director on my occasional leaves. This was another "long turn" and needs a word of explanation. First, for all those years I had a remarkable Key Administrator in Gemma Lum, who had an extremely deft capacity for handling personal and administrative relations and personnel problems. She did this with great oral skill, leaving me to write the more official memoranda, at which I developed some competence. In addition, I had two first-rate Associate Directors: Carolyn Madden for Curriculum and Barbara Dobson for Testing and Certification. Further, in my amateurish, lead-by-example, managing-by-wandering-around style, I was able to let people get on with what they were good at doing. (In fact, one unspoken rule I had as director was: "Always walk the long way round to the bathroom.")

In general, I never had much time for official job descriptions and work study plans, or for frequent performance evaluations. "Why," I used to think, "should we want to constrain people's initiative and creativity in this way? If junior lecturers want to do applied research and product development, why shouldn't they?" A more important reason for my administrative longevity derived from the fact that the English Language Institute—very unusually for an institute of this kind—had its own soft-money resources deriving from test fees and shared-royalty income. So, there was considerable discretionary money at the director's disposal, which, for example, could be used to support conference expenses for those who were not eligible for College general funds. And finally, I developed good working relationships with the College's "budget deans," particularly with the long-serving John Cross, a Professor of Economics. In effect, we could get on with Peter Steiner's aspiration to "rebuild ELI's international reputation," for the most part flying safely and quietly below the College's and the University's radar.

75

A probable mistake

At the end of the 1980s Sue Gass left for Michigan State, leaving a big hole in the teaching of the Program's MA in ESL. The director of the Program's Steering Committee (of which I was a member) argued for discontinuance of the MA and in the ensuing discussions the following points were made. The College of LS & A was more of a PhD-granting place, while the professional schools (such as Business) could rightly focus on master's students. The Graduate School's assessment of student quality relied on measures that favored doctoral entrants since these only consisted of the applicant's grade point average, the quality of the undergraduate university, and the score in the GRE. There was nothing for teaching or work experience, nor indeed any credit for any previous academic publications. Further, the Graduate School said it wasn't in a position to evaluate universities outside the United States, so, in effect, a student coming from Oxford or The Sorbonne was treated the same as one from a technical institute in Garbargistan. All this might not have mattered too much if it was not for the fact that the average student quality score of a degree program determined how much money that program received in student support. Thus, it could be argued that the MA was costing the Program money. It could also be pointed out that a nearby university offered a decent MA in ESL for about a third of the tuition cost of the UM offering.

Privately, I also had concerns about our MA in ESL. Unlike the Aston master's, it was structured around a very standard set of courses without any kind of stand-out specialization. Worse, there did not seem a way of restricting successful applicants to those who had already had some ESL teaching experience (as we had done at Aston); as a result, the classes consisted of a sometimes uncomfortable mix of experienced teachers and those straight from a BA. Because of all these concerns, I did not, in committee, argue for the continuance of the MA as strenuously as I might have done, and the master's was phased out.

In retrospect, my fence-sitting in this regard was a mistake. Applied linguistics at Michigan languished and largely vanished at the doctoral level, even though Joan Morley, with some help from me, was able to develop a successful optional applied track in the BA degree. Although there has been some revival, following the arrival of Diane Larsen-Freeman as ELI Director in 2001, this has taken place through the School of Education (where Diane has tenure), rather than through Linguistics, which, especially since it regained departmental status, was able to attract good quality doctoral applicants in its areas of strength such as phonetics, phonology, syntax, and sociolinguistics. If the MA had been preserved, it would have provided a pool of students, the very best of whom could have been supported, partly through teaching and research in the ELI, at the PhD level. I don't know whether I would have actually succeeded in preserving the MA, but I made a mistake by not sufficiently attempting to do so.

76

Genre Analysis: English in Academic and Research Settings

At the end of the previous chapter, I had noted that I had obtained for my final four months at Aston a period of study leave. This I spent on preparing for the Council's 50th Anniversary Conference, getting ready for Michigan, and starting work on a book contract for Cambridge University Press. The volume that eventually emerged had the title of this episode, but in those early days, I spent my time investigating what others had written about the concept of genre—in folklore studies and cultural anthropology, in literary studies, in the sociology of science, in linguistics, and in rhetoric—as well as in writings in English for Academic Purposes. After moving to Michigan, when time permitted, I plugged away at this manuscript, the last one I would write in longhand on yellow pads, my scratchy efforts being deciphered and then keyboarded onto those old large floppy disks by my long-serving secretary and financial assistant, Rosemary Tackabery.

One new Ann Arbor influence was Alton Becker (although always known in person as "Pete"), a linguistic anthropologist of highly polished thought and writing style. We had many discussions, in particular, about the role of prior texts in shaping communicative products. Here is a bit of Pete:

> It is sometimes felt that prior text can be evoked without an image—that we have an abstract set of 'rules' for an opera or a journal entry—or any of the

language games we can take part in. . . . That seems backwards; one may formulate an abstract image of an opera or a journal entry, full of necessary and probable features, but the act of formulation is itself a language game, in a particular language, and not a prerequisite to understanding opera or journal entries.

I went halfway toward this position; indeed, sometimes we invoke *textual* memories, but at other times we invoke broader, more generic, structures. Pete himself was often full of surprises; for example, one day I asked him if he had ever been rejected by a journal. He looked at me in half-feigned incredulity, "Well, John," he responded, "I have never in my life submitted an article to a journal; sometimes people just ask me to write something, and so I do." Not quite the kind of career management, I had expected! And while we are on the topics of prior texts and textual memories, I should clear up one small misunderstanding. On occasion, over the years, I have been asked why I did not cite the Russian literary theorist Mikhail Bahktin in *Genre Analysis* since there were considerable similarities between some of our ideas. In actual fact, I did not read Bakhtin's classic *The Problem of Speech Genres* (first published in English in 1986) until after I had finished the manuscript. And lest any think I might be claiming some particular credit for independently coming up with comparable thoughts, let me hastily add that Bakhtin had originally had his ideas some 40 years before I did.

In addition to all this reading, thinking, and writing about genre, I had also started to teach a new ELI graduate-level course entitled at that time Dissertation and Proposal Writing. By the fall of 1986, I was ready with an article entitled "Utilizing the Literatures in Teaching the Research Paper," which was published the next year by *TESOL Quarterly*. The middle section of the accompanying abstract adequately summarizes my thinking at that time:

This article outlines and illustrates an approach to the teaching of research English (on a group rather than an individual basis) which derives from four bodies of literature: (a) the sociology of science, (b) citation analysis, (c) technical writing, and (d) English for academic purposes. It is argued that this approach gives the ESL instructor insight into research writing processes and products, increases instructor confidence, provides accessible content, and produces texts from the literatures that can be used directly in class.

Sometime during the winter of 1987–1988, Cambridge University Press began, with increasing vociferousness, to inquire where the completed manuscript was. So, somehow knowing that my "big chance" might be slipping away, I worked away over the next year, eventually producing a text of some 400 manuscript pages. It was divided into four parts, short opening and closing sections called Preliminaries and Applications, respectively, and long middle sections, Part II being entitled Key Concepts and Part III Research-process Genres. The three main concepts were those of discourse community, genre itself, and (language-learning) task. The elaborate definitions of the first two have been much reproduced and discussed, although the former more critically and with less enthusiastic uptake than the latter. In contrast, my fourteen (published) pages on "task" have, as far as I can see, been totally ignored, and this despite much ESL/EAP interest in the 1990s in "task-based learning." So, in a desperate and probably forlorn attempt to rescue my concept of language-learning task from the obscurity in which it has resided for nearly 20 years, here it is again:

> One of a set of differentiated, sequenceable, goal-directed activities drawing upon a range of cognitive and communicative procedures relatable to the acquisition of pre-genre and genre skills appropriate to a foreseen or emerging sociorhetorical situation.

Although this will probably seem somewhat indigestible stripped of the argumentation and illustration that originally surrounded it, it does still come across, I suggest, as a sincere effort to conceive of task as an appropriately *tight* concept. More pragmatically, and as I concluded, "a *genre-centered* approach [to task] is likely to focus student attention on rhetorical action and on the organizational and linguistic means of its accomplishment."

The 1990 *Genre Analysis* volume has been, by some way, the most influential of all my writings. It appeared in CUP's top-of-the-line *Applied Linguistics Series*, is still in print, and has sold more than 10,000 copies. In some ways, it is not so easy to explain its success. It is possible to point to its coverage of disciplinary literatures not at the time likely to fall within the purview of the ESL profession, or to its confident definitional work, or to its reasonable balance between theoretical and practical concerns. However, I believe that the most likely explanation lies in the rhetorical concept of *kairos*, or timeliness. In other words, by around 1990, the worlds of applied discourse analysis, EAP, and academic and research writing were "ready" for a book that attempted to cohere those three worlds. I was lucky in the timing; five years earlier it would have been greeted with puzzlement, and five years later with a yawn.

77

The Birds of Washtenaw County, Michigan,
The University of Michigan Press, 1992

As this episode's title might intimate, the next book-length project was very different, and for this I need to back up a little. Although I had done some incidental birdwatching for much of my life, I only took the hobby up with enthusiasm while in the Sudan in the 1970s. Tony Petitt, the British professor of biology was an expert birdwatcher and, on some hot afternoons, he took me along in his Land Rover to his regular haunts, since the confluence of the Niles in Khartoum was a great place to go bird-watching. Indeed, after a year or so, we even agreed to do a bit of teaching about watching and identifying birds as an extra activity for the international elementary school, which my children were attending. On our first field trip, we piled a dozen or so 10-year-olds into our two vehicles and set off to show them various birding sites around the city, finishing up at the garbage dump because there we could guarantee to find for them the huge, if ugly, Marabou Storks. That evening, it turned out, was a very good time not to have a phone at home. Ambassadors and their wives were apparently calling the school's head teacher and whoever else they could think of to demand an explanation as to why their precious offspring had been taken to the city's insalubrious garbage dump—of all places. In future, we would ask for written permission in advance for any such visits.

I continued to do some birding on occasion while living in Birmingham, but my interest increased greatly when I moved to Michigan, where nearly all the birds were new. After a while, I found myself spending part of the weekends scouring the county's back roads, woods, fields, and lakes looking for birds, and I purchased some primitive software from a guy in California to start creating a database of my bird records. After *Genre Analysis* was in press, I started casting around for another writing project and soon discovered that two other people had even more detailed and comprehensive county records of birds: Mike Kielb, perhaps the city's leading birder and working at that time as a research associate in the Faculty of Medicine, and Dick Wolinski, an ecologist who worked for a bio-engineering company. In the summer of 1990, we began to meet whenever we could to plan what would become *The Birds of Washtenaw County, Michigan* and would be published by the University of Michigan Press in 1992. Mike inputted everything into the recalcitrant PageMaker program and did all the bar-charts, tables, and histograms; I took charge of collating the records; and Dick wrote the geographical and topographical introduction. We largely co-wrote the bulk of the book, which consisted mainly of a Site Guide and about 260 Species Accounts. This wasn't to be a field guide or a picture book, but a careful quantitative compilation, as this extract from the opening page demonstrates:

> In essence, we wanted to provide an up-to-date and comprehensive account of the bird-life in Washtenaw County as it was known towards the close of the twentieth century. More specifically, we wanted to provide the best answers we could to such questions as:
>
> - When, if at all, is a particular species likely to occur in the county?
> - How common (or easy to find) is that species and how does its frequency of occurrence vary during the year?

- In what kind of habitat is it most likely to occur?
- What would be a good place in the county to look for it?

And to round out the picture, here is a typical short species account:

Eastern Phoebe *Sayornis phoebe*
Finding Code: 5
Fairly uncommon migrant and uncommon summer resident
Spring arrival: 13 March (1989)
Late fall date: 25 October (1989)
Maximum: 6 on 3 October 1987 at Eberwhite Woods

The Eastern Phoebe is the earliest of the flycatchers to return to Washtenaw County and the last to depart. As a migrant the dark-headed tail-pumping phoebe can be seen in a wide variety of habitats, but as a summer resident it is most likely found near bridges over streams and creeks, since it has the habit of nesting under these man-made structures.

The appearance of *BOWM* (as it became known) had one important effect. Prior to 1992, the considerable numbers of county birdwatchers had spent most of their birding time at various "hot spots" in southeastern Michigan and nearby Ontario. After 1992, however, interest became much more local as the birding community attempted to update and modify the records we had summarized. (Could a phoebe be found as late as November?)

I continued to bird on a regular basis, both in Washtenaw, and, when time allowed, on my fairly frequent conference or speaking trips to other parts of the world. For instance, four of us, three professors of linguistics (Pete Becker, Jim Milroy, and myself, plus Chip Tamason, a neighbor of mine) would have regular morning outings; in the winter months, we would all wear cheap Chinese fur hats and so became known as "the rabbitheads."

My birdwatching hobby began to be known among the EAP community and, in later years, sometimes the local hosts would try to accommodate my interests. One of the most memorable of these occurred when I was invited to give a plenary talk at a conference in Okayama, Japan. On the birdwatching morning, I waited as instructed in the hotel lobby. First to arrive were four gentlemen in dark suits in two black cars, none of whom spoke a word of English. These apparently were the representatives of Okayama Prefecture, presumably looking forward to a morning away from the office. Next to come were two young women in high heels, who announced that they were the translators. Finally, two birdwatchers showed up, neither of whom again spoke any English. So, we all set off for the local park and its famous garden (ranked number three in Japan, I was told). The main birdwatcher and I managed to communicate through the pictures and the Japanese bird-name transliterations in my *Birds of Japan* field-guide, so we didn't need the translators very much. After an hour or so, I managed to identify an uncommon female flycatcher, which impressed the lead birdwatcher. When the walk around the pleasant park was over, a long conversation broke out between the birdwatcher and the prefecture gentlemen, including some urgent-seeming cell phone calls. It turned out that the birdwatcher, impressed by my small skills, wanted to take me to the best birding places in the city, which, of course, turned out to be the garbage dump and the sewage farm. Eventually, permission was granted and off we went. When we arrived, the birdwatchers and I set off, but the translators refused to get out of the car, and the city officials never left the safe footing of the car park.

During my time off in Okayama, I also did some birdwatching on my own, and wherever I went, small boys on bicycles would shout "birdwatcher" at me as they passed. In the end, I found out why. There was apparently an annual televised contest held in a baseball stadium for the best Japanese pop song of the year. Before the advent of electronic voting, votes were counted in the following way. Each member of the audience in the stadium was given a piece of white cardboard and a marker pen. After the thirty or so pop songs had been performed, the audience wrote the number of their favorite song on the board. At this point, 30 birdwatchers with binoculars trooped on stage and faced the assembled multitude, one to count all the Number 1s, the next the number 2s, and so on. In this way, Japanese birders used to have their yearly moment of fame, and hence knowledge of this English word was acquired by the passing boys.

In the years since 1992, I have written one or two articles about birds for the state journal, *Michigan Birds and Natural History*, and more recently I have become very interested in Michigan butterflies. Sometimes people ask me about those hobbies and whether there is any relationship between these interests and my interests in discourses. I suspect that any connection might go like this: Both areas involve some integration of eye, ear, and brain (though in very different ways) and both involve some searching for patterns in the data. In fact, quite a number of discourse analysts are keen birdwatchers, including Guy Cook, Florence Davies, Peter Fries, and Evelyn Hatch. So I keep birding on my academic trips and I keep some sort of world species list, which currently stands at about 1,400 species (some 15 percent of all the birds in the world). I have hopes of reaching 1,500 before the Grim Reaper takes away my bins.

78

A return to teaching materials

After the fancy footwork of *Genre Analysis* and the hobbyist enthusiasms of the bird book, it was time to direct my attention to the business of consolidating EAP classroom and study materials. As it happened, Carolyn Madden, the Associate Director for Curriculum in the ELI, and I had started a new line of textbooks with the University of Michigan Press entitled the "Michigan Series in English for Academic & Professional Purposes." So, one day Carolyn came to me and said, "Why don't you work with Chris Feak (a lecturer specializing in teaching academic writing) and produce a writing textbook for the series? But you and Chris have a very different status, and both of you are pretty hardheaded and obstinate, so I think it would be best if you had a project assistant to keep you from each other's throats and act as mediator whenever necessary." And, indeed, the early days weren't easy, but once Chris and I realized that the assistant was actually making things worse rather than better, we started to collaborate on a more equal basis. Although Chris believes—and has written—that she felt she was in an apprentice-master relationship, I actually thought of myself more as an "enabler" or an "encourager" of a talented junior colleague. Even if Chris didn't always see it that way.

A good working relationship began to develop when we agreed that Chris would have primary responsibility for certain units and I would look after certain others. Chris has preserved some of my comments on one of her drafts, and their tone is perhaps indicative:

> This section seems too swift. Can you slow it down as you did in the previous section? Students will need time to digest this.

> Do you think we could expand this explanation to address writing for publication? You might want to refer to our discussion in unit 8.

> This section needs a lead-in; otherwise it seems to go against our earlier advice.

Chris commented many years later: "The use of *our*, *we*, and *us* certainly gave the impression we were collaborating when in fact this was John's subtle way of revealing the strategies of an old-timer and helping a newcomer understand the 'tricks of the trade', while making her feel a part of the trade." Even so, I still don't see it exactly that way.

Academic Writing for Graduate Students (AWG) was published in 1994, with a second edition (mostly done by Chris) ten years later. It has been a commercial and critical success, and is today one of the Press's bestsellers. It is both suitably "tasky" and has a clear structure. As we stated in the introduction to the first edition:

> AWG is organized into eight units. The first three units are essentially preparatory; they prepare the way for the more genre-specific activities in later units. Unit One presents an overview of the considerations involved in successful academic writing, with a deliberate stress on early exposure to

the concept of positioning. Units Two and Three deal with two overarching patterns in English expository prose: the movement from general to specific and the movement from problem to solution. Unit Four acts as a crucial link between the earlier and later units, since it deals with how to handle the discussion of data. Units Five and Six deal with writing summaries and critiques respectively. . . . Finally, Units Seven and Eight deal with constructing a real research paper, that is, one that might be submitted for publication.

Chris and I would publish a more advanced sequel in 2000, but this was less commercially successful, and, in the spring of 2009, two small super-advanced volumes—one on writing abstracts and the other on writing reviews of the literature—were published. Chris and I now share the editorship of the EAPP series, and we have developed an excellent working relationship with the Press's dynamic and highly successful ESL Editor, Kelly Sippell. Meanwhile, Chris, who still remains a lecturer, has developed a remarkable career in her own right as an expert in research writing and writing for publication—as a provider of workshops, as an overseas specialist for the State Department, and as a plenary speaker. For example, she gave one of the three plenaries at the 2009 BALEAP conference held at the University of Reading in the UK. Chris's rise to prominence in the ESP/EAP field (she is now a member of the editorial board of *The English for Specific Purposes Journal*) is one of the developments I take most pride in.

79

The Michigan Corpus of Academic Spoken English

In the summer of 1997 Sarah Briggs of the Testing and Certification Division and I had an interesting conversation. She said that the growing interest in corpora (i.e., electronic databases of language samples) was something that should also be of interest to the division. In particular a spoken corpus of academic speech would be valuable not only for tests of academic listening comprehension, but also for future EAP developments. We discussed this further and we agreed that the division could fund a major development in this area, using some of its by-now-considerable test fee income. We hired Rita Simpson, who had recently completed a PhD at Michigan in sociolinguistics, as Project Manager and the Michigan Corpus of Academic Spoken English (MICASE) was born. Rita, Sarah, and I spent some considerable time devising and revising the shape of the corpus so that it would provide a representative microcosm of the speech events that students (of various kinds) would encounter and participate in. Anna Mauranen, an outstanding Finnish discourse analyst, was recruited as an external consultant, and she too contributed to the corpus compilation debate. Looking back, I think we got it mostly right, even if, in the end, the Business School and the Faculty of Medicine were underrepresented.

We employed several linguistics undergraduates as part-time assistants and they did the bulk of the recording and transcribing. In 1988, the digital services unit of the Graduate Library graciously agreed to fund the development of a "Web-based search interface so that MICASE would be available not only to researchers at Michigan but to student teachers, and researchers around the world." We also knew that creating a spoken corpus of 1.8 million words divided among 152 speech events would be a costly undertaking, and that we had no real hope of recouping more than a small percentage of our expenses. In these circumstances, we decided to make it available to everybody for free—a decision that has been universally applauded, except perhaps by my own dean. The construction, distribution and use of MICASE would, I think, have greatly pleased the ELI's founding director, Charles Fries, whose classic 1952 volume, *The Structure of English*, was based on 50 hours of transcribed telephone conversations.

One day Rita Simpson said to me, "I think, John, your involvement in MICASE as faculty advisor has given you a new lease of life." This now strikes me as very true, since my long-running interest in primarily written texts was doubtless becoming a little jaded. I began to learn what kinds of questions could be asked of an electronic database (via a concordance program) and what kinds of questions should be avoided.

However, I never became a corpus linguist *per se*, rather one of a growing band of individuals who use corpora to provide authentic examples or to test out intuitions and hypotheses. I also enjoyed working with young people, particularly the undergraduate research assistants, and since 1999 I have co-presented and co-authored two or three papers with them. Many more much shorter joint studies are hosted on the ELI's home page. As of October 2008, MICASE data has been used in more than 70 publications and in six PhD dissertations, while MICASE-based conference presentations certainly run into three figures. So, the project has been a considerable success, and one way we know this comes from the messages we receive from around the world when the web interface goes down, often from concerned students facing deadlines for their MICASE-based projects. Rita Simpson left for California a few years ago, but corpus linguistics remains a very lively area at the ELI with several staff being employed; Rita was ably replaced as director first by Annelie Adel and now by Ute Römer.

80

The North University Building (NUB)

Until the building was demolished in 2001, the ELI occupied the top floor of NUB. Below the institute was the University Herbarium, with its massive collection of dried plant specimens, and below that, on the ground floor, one of the university's main computer centers. I was long struck by this odd juxtaposition of three different communities, and I had long thought it would make an excellent site for a dissertation in discourse analysis. However, I failed to find anybody interested in conducting such a study, so in the end I decided I would like to do it myself. The result was the 1998 book *Other Floors—Other Voices: A Textography of a Small University Building*. I coined the term *textography* because the exploration turned out to be more than a discourse analysis but less than an ethnography. It took me four years, even with a couple of occasional research assistants, and, because of certain interpersonal entanglements en route, probably would not in the end have made an easily "doable" dissertation topic. The one extract I have chosen to illustrate *Other Floors* deals with the different speed of the "clocks" on the three floors:

> ... The "communities of practice" ... in the North University Building also have their separate and highly temporal rhythms. This tempo is *allegro assai* in the Computer Resource Site, for the consultants often function like text-recovery paramedics in some discoursal Emergency Room. There are pressing urgencies here, as in the prototypical "My computer just ate my disk, and I have to turn in my paper by five o'clock—please help me!" Upstairs in the Herbarium, the tempo is *lentissimo*, because the tangible return on the loaning and gifting of specimens in the form of either expert "determinations" or published treatments may be, as we shall see, a matter of many years. Although the physical rhythms are expeditious enough, with a fair amount of walking about, and with a palpable sense of deft movement in the assemblying and disassemblying of sets of specimens, the horizons of expectation in terms of outcome can be immensely long. Finally, on the top floor, the observer will experience a steadier *adagio* pace in which the set examination "seasons" have the regular repetitive quality of agricultural practice.

As perhaps this extract shows, *Other Floors* was an idiosyncratic work, and I have never done anything similar either before or since. It was a commercial failure, but something of a critical success. (I suppose I would rather have it that way round.) Total sales amounted to little more than 500 copies, but there were also comments (from Greg Myers) like this:

> In this study, Swales can give free rein to his long-standing love of the overlooked genre and unexpected insight, in his descriptions of signs in the Computing Resource Site, or the herbarium specimen sheets, or the royalty agreement for an ELT textbook series. But the book isn't just offbeat details; in the last chapter he redeems his pledge to come back to the issue of whether 'discourse community' remains a useful concept. He reviews the

debates critically, giving enough description and quotation of earlier studies for readers new to the issues and far from a library. And he offers a definition of the 'Place Discourse Community' that looks less like the 'Invisible College' of the sociology of scientific knowledge, and more like the very visible offices, units, and teams with whom we share corridors, pigeonholes, and photocopiers. He replaces the polarity of global and local (with its implied evaluation) with a different contrast between communities constituted by their focus on a goal and communities constituted by place.

81

ELI 620/621 and Linguistics 429

For most of my teaching career at Michigan, my two most regular courses were Dissertation Writing and Writing for Publication I and II (ELI 620/621) and Discourse Analysis and Language Learning Materials (Linguistics 429). The ELI courses were designed for senior doctoral students, but on occasion there were also master's students writing theses, native speakers, and the occasional visiting scholar. These participants (my preferred term) could come from any of the university's 19 colleges; as a result, one challenge was to try and form them into a socio-rhetorical community, a support group for each other. Tactics for this included academic humor and parody, "Utilizing the literatures" (Episode 76), exchanges of experiences, social get-togethers such as a pot-luck at my house, their "academic news of the week" (if any) at the beginning of each class, and lots of rhetorical consciousness-raising and informal genre analysis. I also took them behind the scenes into the "occluded" worlds of recommendations, applications and evaluations, making use when I could of my own experiences. I tried to get the participants to view disciplinary texts (including their own) from something like the detached perspective of the discourse analyst. Although I had regular individual meetings with participants to work on their texts, it soon became clear to me that my role in these classes was not so much to improve their written products, but to improve them as *writers* of academic English. Any skills and insights acquired in 620/621 would need to be transferable to future contexts.

It is sometimes argued that classes at this level need to be discipline-specific. While there is some merit in this argument, there is also merit in an argument for participant heterogeneity. In the latter context, there is quick recognition that there is little point in arguing about the *content* of the exemplars, so that attention is drawn to its linguistic surfaces. More important, being exposed by a class member to a very different (disciplinary) culture, say pharmacology, can offer valuable insights into your own (say education). And here it is worth remembering that many of my participants had been spending three or four years deeply embedded in the labs, research group meetings, articles, and conferences of their own disciplinary micro-worlds. They were often "ready" to hear of and read about other academic experiences and trajectories. Indeed, when, in the first meeting, I used to make much of the fact that this class was precious to me because it constituted, for my own research purposes, my "laboratory," this gave me, I believe, enhanced face validity in their eyes. These courses were both enjoyable and successful, and have been taken over, with great success, by my colleague, Christine Feak. When I started these courses in the late 1980s, Michigan was one of very few institutions to offer such courses, one of the handful of others being UCLA. Today such courses are proliferating across the world of research universities. Another source of satisfaction.

My 429 "capstone" course in the Applied Linguistics sub-concentration for a BA in Linguistics took time to take its final shape, but, in its latter years, extramurally, it included a working breakfast at my house for the fifteen or so participants, and two "field trips." One was to the "Rare Books" section of the main library, where they could peruse language-teaching textbooks from the past and from many different cultures (including a 17th-century book in Latin for teaching Persian). A favorite with those students with political leanings was an early 20th-century small book produced by a trade union in New York designed to teach recent immigrants terminology such as *strike, worker solidarity,* and *scab*. One year a left-leaning undergraduate expressed a strong desire to purchase a copy on the web, but gave up when the Rare Books librarian told him that there were only seven known copies of this text in existence! The other "field trip" was to the UM Press where the estimable Kelly Sippell would demonstrate to the students the arduous process of turning an ESL manuscript into a textbook. Another eye-opener, I believed.

The final projects for 429 consisted on some piece of original discourse analysis with a view to its pedagogical exploitation. I arranged for these to be presented in either conference paper or poster format to the members of the ELI in late April. We typically started at 10:00 and finished with pizzas at 12:30, and I here I would like to express my gratitude to all the members of the institute who willingly attended and participated in these events. The students were variously unnerved, excited, and impressed by having to display their projects to a substantial "real audience," rather than a captive collection of classmates. Luckily, the Michigan undergraduates typically over-achieved, especially with the data they managed to collect, and Barbara Dobson and I managed to recruit some excellent junior research assistants in testing from these classes. I have to say, however, that I was somewhat unnerved by some of the comments on the official evaluation forms, such as, "This is the first time I have been treated as a grown-up in any of my Michigan classes" or "In my last semester, I am finally doing a serious research project. Thank you." While such comments were personally welcome, they did raise broader systematic issues in my mind about their undergraduate experiences elsewhere.

82

The year 2004

With the page budget for this memoir (of sorts) rapidly shrinking, I will focus mainly in this final entry for Chapter Six on the *annus mirabilis* of 2004. The year started in January with a visit to snowy Uppsala near Stockholm for the award of an honorary PhD. For this very classy event, I was accompanied by my companion, my sister, and a cousin.

For the ceremony, mostly in Latin, I was dressed up, for the first time in my life, in white tie and tails—although my rented patent leather shoes pinched terribly so that I winced around the stage of the grand University Hall while collecting my degree. At the key moments of the awards, the Swedish army fired off a cannon outside. A very impressive touch, we thought. My selection for this distinction was largely the work of a long-standing colleague, Britt-Louise Gunnarsson, the Professor of Scandinavian Languages at Uppsala, and, for whom, later that year, I would be publishing an article on the discourse of art criticism for her sixtieth birthday *Festschrift*.

Two books were published in 2004; the first was the second edition of *AWG*, with Chris Feak doing more than her fair share of the rethinking, updating, and rewriting. In consequence, I thought it only proper that Chris should become the first author, but Kelly Sippell of the UM Press thought that this was not a good idea from a marketing point of view. So, instead, we tilted the royalties in Chris' favor. The second was a sequel to *Genre Analysis* called *Research Genres: Explorations and Applications*, again published by Cambridge in its Applied Linguistics Series. In this, I was, *inter alia*, able to make use of the MICASE data, producing chapters on research group meetings and dissertation defenses. By the first years of the new century, the relevant literature had grown exponentially and the bibliography eventually extended to some 420 items. I will not attempt the like again. The production process, which went through the New York rather than the Cambridge (UK) office was also a bit of trial. The original copy editor, for example, insisted that I couldn't use *on the other hand* without having used *on the one hand*, despite my demonstration, based on Ken Hyland's corpus of research articles, that the former was six times more frequent than the latter. On the whole, *Research Genres* has done reasonably well, but it has not been picked up quite as much as I had anticipated, or in such extensive ways as I had hoped.

In February, I was in Zaragoza, Spain, giving a two-day doctoral seminar and firming up the good relationship we had with the English Department there (which still continues). I was also appointed a "researcher of excellence" at the University of Zaragoza, and thereby was given a substantial pile of Euros. A return visit to Aston University (on my way to a conference in Belfast) was a rather different occasion because, on arrival, I discovered that my old Language Studies Unit was about to be closed down, ostensibly for financial reasons. When Julian Edge introduced me he said something like: "Here is John Swales who gave almost the first talk ever given at the LSU, and now is here to certainly give its last."

In October I was back in Santiago, Chile, and in December to Copenhagen to give an invited "gala" lecture in honor of Inger Lassen of Aalborg University, who was being awarded the Hedorf Prize for distinguished studies of business discourse. This had come about because in 2000 I had spent a semester at the Aarhus Business School as a visiting professor. The members of my small fifth-year class were, not unexpectedly, focused on business communications for their final projects, and I got to know Inger and her work on business and professional discourses, since she was working at Aalborg, just a hundred miles or so to the north. Anyway, one of the perks of the Prize was that the recipient could choose a speaker to give the 30-minute "gala lecture" (a new subgenre for me) and she chose me. I was told by the organizer that the audience would consist of the prize winner and members of her family, business executives, trade unionists, and various academics, so would I take this into account as I prepared? So doing, I chose to finish with the following (which had circulated on email some years before). I entitled it "the job applicant's revenge" and then revealed it part by part on the overheads:


```
Charles E. Carpenter
Director, Human Resources

Dear Chuck,

Thank you for your letter of April 17. However, after
careful consideration, I regret to inform you that I am
unable to accept your refusal to offer me employment with
your company.
```

> This year has been exceptional in that I have received an unusually large number of rejection letters. In such a circumstance, it has proved impossible for me to accept all refusals.
>
> Despite your company's outstanding qualifications and previous experience in rejecting applicants, I find that your rejection does not meet with my needs at the present time. Therefore, I will initiate employment with your company immediately following graduation. I look forward to seeing you then.
>
> Best of luck in rejecting future candidates.
>
> Sincerely

It brought the house down—it always does—and so provided a suitably gala-like ending to the talk.

I officially retired in June 2006, which was celebrated (if that is the word) by a delightful retirement conference in my honor, largely organized by Rita Simpson. Several of the people who have been featured in these pages, such as Tony Dudley-Evans and Ann Johns, attended. Also present were three of the four members of the original Doctoral Group, who, at the final dinner, gave me a fair old roasting with a skit entitled *John's calling*, which included a replay of the incident in Episode 73 where I had inadvertently described my own writing as "brilliant."

As it turned out, I was asked by the Dean to come back as acting Director of the ELI for the first half of 2007, when the outgoing director, Diane Larsen-Freeman, had a six-month study leave. Little did I know when I accepted the interim position that the institute would have to move buildings in April of that year! And even after that, I have been in the office most of the working days of the week, working on the transcripts from the "Swales Conference," preparing textbooks with Chris, writing blurbs, forewords and afterwords for sundry volumes. (Nowadays, I largely inhabit the blurbosphere.) As Albert Markwardt wrote of Charles Fries, the ELI's founding director, "retirement is just a word."

SEVEN

Reflections on an Educational Life

83

A few meta-reflections

I am sufficiently aware of contemporary work on text and discourse analysis to recognize that the vignettes recounted in the previous chapters are not, in any simple sense, "true slices of an educational life." After all, some I have recounted before in oral form, and in these retellings they become shaped in some more artful way, and have been reshaped again as I have been putting them down on paper. They have in effect been multiply "re-voiced." And, of course, they are egocentric, rather than offering some triangulated inter-subjective account of events. Consider the case of the schoolboy episode, the one which I entitled "A touch of *realpolitic*" and where I offered the view that the headmaster could do little other than not expel me from the school because of the administrative vacuum that would have ensued. In fact, of course, his reasons might have been quite different, such as fear of litigation or a desire to support my housemaster. Doubtless, similar alternative interpretations could apply to various other incidents.

On a more troubling level, there emerges the question raised by the cultural anthropologist, Charles Bauman: In what sense is it the case that the events make the narrative (as one might expect at first sight), or is it also the case that the narrative makes the events? After all, there has been, on my part, much careful selection of certain details (such as a fragment of conversation), and much omission of other details. Perhaps, we can leave the issue here with two quotations. The first from the Franco-Bulgarian textual theorist, Tzvetan Todorov:

> No narrative is natural; a choice and a construction will always preside over its appearance; narrative is a discourse, not a series of events. There exists no 'proper' narrative as opposed to 'figurative' ones (just as there is no 'proper' meaning); all narratives are figurative.

The second from Ilya Prigogine, who won the Nobel prize for chemistry: "On all levels reality implies an essential element of conceptualization." Or, as I have recounted above, reconceptualization.

Despite these equivocations, it also remains the case that the episodes recounted in the previous six chapters are not, in the end, fictions. They are all anchored in some version of reality at least as perceived and then presented by their raconteur. So, with that, let's move on to somewhere else.

84

At the end of the accounts

I have been a classroom teacher in university settings for 47 years now, and still enjoy its challenges. (Grading papers is another matter.) There has also been a long (if small) administrative career, and only once was I subject to an official complaint about my management, and even there the outcome was not resolved in the complainant's favor. I do not work in a glamorous or high-profile field, one that might require brilliance and/or remarkable erudition on the part of its leading protagonists. Rather, my corner of Applied Linguistics is a field that rewards concentration, persistence, and an appropriate degree of educational self-questioning. So, in this accounting, I have tried to interweave into a personal history various kinds of excursions that may have, at least for some, a certain pedagogical or investigative resonance.

The story itself has been oddly serendipitous, one of being uncannily in the right place and the right time, so that it would serve ill as a model "career trajectory" for younger colleagues. A part of this serendipity comes from my choice of the field of English for Academic and Research Purposes, because knowledge of this variety of English has, throughout my working lifetime, become increasingly *de rigeur* for all those millions of academics, researchers, and research students who have not had the benefit of acquiring English as first language. International anxiety here about potential deficits is sharp, and alas often now reinforced by all those national evaluation criteria prioritizing publication in peer-reviewed English-language journals. In consequence, I have, over a working lifetime, visited 50 countries to speak about such issues. It was luck that placed me in charge of materials production at the College of Engineering in Libya in the late sixties, and it was the fortuitous timing of the Libyan Revolution of 1969 that led to the publication of *Writing Scientific English* in 1971.

I do not intend here to inflict upon the reader any kind of numerical accounting of the numbers of books, articles, or exemplars of other genres that I have written or co-written. Suffice to say, there has been quite a lot of them, even if in fact the total output would not be dissimilar to that of many other senior professors here at the University of Michigan. A few items, particularly *Genre Analysis*, have achieved a certain prominence; many others have been noticed in some smaller way; and an unfortunate few have fallen into the scholastic black hole of never having been cited. As many have noted, we authors often reserve a soft spot for such failed works, and so the final extract from my writing will be from one of these—perhaps in a last desperate attempt to resuscitate a textual corpse.

In the *Genre Analysis* episode I noted that Mikhail Bahktin's *The Problem of Speech Genres and Other Late Essays* did not appear in English until 1986, nearly 40 years after most of it had originally been written in Russian. So, for a small, occasional piece published in 2000, I wrote an alternative-universe fantasy of what might have been the consequences *if* the *Speech Genres* essay had been smuggled out of the Soviet Union and published in the West in the early 1950s. Here is the close:

Afterword

That history, as I said, at the outset of this small reminiscence, does not now need to be retold in any detail. But perhaps I should remind anybody who might read these few pages of just a few of the facts. Bakhtin's *The Problem of Speech Genres,* as it was finally called, was published in the same year and by the same press as Ludwig Wittgenstein's *Philosophical Investigations,* and these two seminal works have been linked in the thoughts of the world's intelligentsia ever since. They remain, despite the academic industries that have grown up around them, tantalizingly similar and tantalizingly different. However, Language Sciences really shot to its current pre-eminence with the appearance in 1964 of *Aspects of a Theory of Language and Social Life* by Noam Chomsky and Erving Goffman. Within a space of ten years, a Nobel Prize in Language Sciences had been established, and fittingly the first laureate was Mikhail Bakhtin, although he was too frail to travel to Stockholm to receive it. Instead, it was presented to him at his retirement home in Klimovsk, where he made his last public utterance, this time about dialogism and religious practice. Later laureates were, of course, Chomsky and then Halliday, the latter for his masterpiece *Context in Text and Text in Context.* There is doubtless more to say, but the hour grows late and the cat is scratching at the door.

So, here is another *Afterword,* a genre I am increasingly familiar with these days. Although a fanciful dream, it does once again show how many things might have been different if just one thing had been other than it was. The only responses I received following the appearance of the piece in *Written Communication* were a couple of emails from English Department graduate students somewhere in the U.S. hinterland, congratulating me on having written a lively narrative rather than a typical dull exposition; alas, it seemed all too obvious from their messages that they believed my little fairy story to have been literally true.

More broadly, there have been many satisfactions in my life, one being that as I have passed from one educationist decade to the next most aspects of my professional life have improved. But there have also been some dissatisfactions. I regret, for example, never having put sufficient effort into learning good Arabic or good French. Much more significantly, while I am grateful to the University of Michigan for being "big enough" to offer someone without an earned doctorate a tenured professorship, the university has always, I suspect, thought of me as some kind of exceptional case. And when I "officially" retired, it was made very clear that there would be no tenure-track replacement for my area of interest and expertise. Indeed, across the English-speaking world, the number of senior people working in English for Academic or Research Purposes is pathetically small, and perhaps even shrinking (as at Michigan). Although the situation is somewhat better in other regions, such as Scandinavia, Southern Europe, and Latin America, a general failure to develop proper career structures (along with their associated "respectability") in an educational enterprise central to contemporary international research and scholarship remains my greatest disappointment.

85

"Who can know the dancer from the dance?"

I have long thought that this famous line from W. B. Yeats is a wonderful metaphor for comparing the impact of style versus substance, or to subvert one of Chomsky's famous distinctions, for assessing the relative importance of performance vis-a-vis competence. Assuming, for the sake of argument, that I have had a fairly successful academic career, how much of that influence might be ascribed to what I have had to say, and how much to the way I have learned to say it? Of course, this is a more severe disjunction than reality would attest, but let it stand for the moment. One point of departure is to note my penchant for self-criticism—"to make pre-emptive strikes against myself, partly to move the agenda forward and partly to show that there is life in the old dog yet."

This was a trope I think I assimilated from my undergraduate philosophy days, for philosophers are more prone than other academics to revisit and correct their earlier positions. However, a more memorable instance occurred when I went in the 1970s to a linguistics conference in England, where one of the main speakers was the well-known semanticist, John Lyons. From the buzz of conversation in the room as we waited for the Great Man to arrive, it was clear that he had said something very odd in his latest publication about the relationship of *sentence* to *utterance.* Anyway, he marched up to the podium and immediately began by saying something like, "First, I would like to make it clear that what I have recently written about *sentence* and *utterance* was seriously wrong. What I should have said was . . . ." As he said this, you could sense the air deflating from the assembled Young Turks, who up until that moment had been bent upon raising objections to his published position. I sensed that day that academic confessions could be thoroughly disarming.

As it happens, Ken Hyland published in 2008 an article on my writing. Among other points, he notes the stance I have described in the previous paragraph, commenting on how often "explicit self-mention is used in a self-deprecatory way." He adds, "Swales employs hedges and mitigation throughout his work, opening a discursive space which invites readers into a dialogue where they can consider and dispute his interpretations." He observes my heavy use of adjectives, usually evaluative and usually positively so, and reflects on my apparent fondness for "a slightly quaint and dated reference to *'the reader'*." (Sometimes I think I overdo the reader stuff as well as use too many adjectives.) Here is one of his conclusions, "In some ways, John's prose style recalls other ways of talking about knowledge which perhaps tempers the influence of the empirical social sciences with the more reflective traditions of the humanities as he introduces us to the ideas he has encountered and shaped from thinkers who do not fit neatly into our discipline."

As I reflect on Ken's analysis of the "Swales Corpus," I am first reminded of something that Tim Johns used to say in our Birmingham days in the 1980s: "A good writer is one who makes a friend of his or her reader," and, as much as anything, that is what I am still trying to do. Second, with reference to this episode's opening disjunctive question, I can do no better than repeat an observation that I have made at least once before: In my line of business, "a good teller of a tale can become a teller of a good tale." However, there naturally needs to be some sort of tale to start with.

86

Two endings

The first book I read with two endings was John Fowles' *The French Lieutenant's Woman*, and back in the 1970s, this late modernist device made a lasting impression on me; sufficiently lasting for me to attempt a similar close to *Incidents in an Educational Life*. The first ending comes from the "Little Gidding" section of T.S.Eliot's "The Four Quartets":

> *Ash on an old man's sleeve*
> *Is all the ash the burnt roses leave.*
> *Dust in the air suspended*
> *Marks the place where a story ended.*

Readers who know me personally will realize the particularity of the opening line. But the story is, in fact, not quite ended . . . .

In November 2008 I reached my 70th birthday, an event I tried to ensure would pass off relatively quietly since, in the immediately preceding years, there had been quite enough fuss. Later in 2008, I went to give the opening plenary at a small specialized conference on academic discourse at Jaca in the Pyrennean foothills, and then to Barcelona to lead two workshops, en route to see my daughter and her family in the south of France. In Fall 2008, I offered an informal seminar for four engaging students from the university's joint doctoral program in English and education. At the time of writing (January 2009), I anticipate that that will have been my last class. In 2009, I have been invited to examine to be the external examiner for a Canadian PhD and have accepted invitations to speak in Argentina, Brazil, and China. In the meantime, my three co-authors and I have just started work on the long-delayed second edition of *The Birds of Washtenaw County, Michigan*. Also, there are more further advanced textbooks to be co-written for the University of Michigan Press, one on publishing research articles and the other devoted to academic communications (editorial correspondence, applications, recommendations, and the like). And Kelly Sippell is already talking about a third edition of *Academic Writing for Graduate Students*. For the foreseeable future, I will be going regularly to my office in the ELI, working on various projects, and using the remains of my research account to support part-time research assistants. I retain the optimism of the mediaeval mystic, Juliana of Norwich, and her famous invocation, "All shall be well, and all shall be well, and all manner of thing shall be well," but somewhere down the road there will be a place where an educational story ended.